h

and lives in Manchester.

Also by Noddy Holder

Who's Crazee Now? My Autobiography

The World According to Noddy

Noddy Holder

Constable • London

CONSTABLE

First published in Great Britain by Constable, 2014
This edition published in the UK by Constable, 2015

1 3 5 7 9 10 8 6 4 2

A CIP catalogue record for this book
is available from the British Library.

ISBN 978-1-47211-967-4 (paperback)
ISBN: 978-1-47211-565-2 (ebook)

Typeset in Great Britain by
SX Composing DTP, Rayleigh, Essex

Printed and bound in Great Britain by CPI Group (UK) Ltd,
Croydon, CR0 4YY

Constable
is an imprint of
Constable & Robinson Ltd

100 Victoria Embankment
London EC4Y 0DY

An Hachette UK Company

www.hachette.co.uk

www.constablerobinson.com

To Suzan for leaving me bewitched, bothered and bewildered.

To Charisse, Jessica, Django and Isabelle for just being wonderful, marvellous and caring for me.

To Frasier, Columbo, Ed B and the late Reg P for never failing to make me smile, smile, smile.

CONTENTS

INTRODUCTION

What can you say about Noddy Holder that hasn't been said before? I'd better think of something as I've been asked to write 500 words and 'What can you say about Noddy Holder that hasn't been said before?' is 488 words short.

In all seriousness, I'm very proud to call Noddy my friend. There are still times when we go for a pizza together, usually around five (it has been known for us to be the only two people in the restaurant), and I look at him telling another great anecdote and think: 'You really are Noddy Holder.' I grew up idolizing him because Slade were serious musicians and Noddy was the owner of not only one of the best rock voices ever to come out of England but also one of the best hats. They made a string of the most perfect pop singles you will ever hear. They were rock gods, pop stars and style icons (except for Dave Hill's 'Metal Nun' outfit), and yet strangely touchable. They were living the life we all wanted to lead but no one resented their success: they retained a bond with the common idiot. When Nod was on *Top of the Pops* you always felt that the world was a better place for having Noddy in it.

I've often thought that it must be great being Noddy, and not just because the 'Merry Xmas Everybody' cheque drops through his letterbox every April. Everywhere Nod goes, people are really pleased to see him. I can't even say that in my own house. Just the other day, after another pizza (taken at the daringly late hour of six), an ageing taxi driver wearing a Hawkwind *In Search of Space* T-shirt accosted us in a state of high excitement. 'Noddy,' he expostulated, waving an outstretched hand, 'great to meet you. You were a massive part of my childhood. And you, Mark.' (As he looked even older than me, this seemed unlikely, unless he was flushing my head down the toilet at Markland Hill Primary School.)

That's typical of the reaction Noddy gets. People genuinely adore him. He really is that most overused of phrases: 'a national treasure'. I've spent a great deal of time with him: on stage, on the radio, supping pints, buying guitars, eating pizza. He's never less than great company and one of the nicest guys I know. Mind you, I do hang out with a lot of evil criminal masterminds. I'm proud to know Nod, and hopefully you'll know him a bit better after reading this book. Now read on and learn from one of the modern world's great thinkers (possibly an exaggeration but what the heck). Welcome to the world according to Noddy ...

Mark Radcliffe, Knutsford City Limits, 2014

Chapter One

DIRTY LAUNDRY

Staff who work in Poundland shops say the question they are most often asked is 'How much is this ...?'

It's a POUND shop for £*?!'s sake!

The question I'm most often asked is 'Will you ever get back with Slade?'

I left the band twenty-three years ago and yet people are still curious.

So once and for all here's my answer: 'Will I ever get back with Slade? ...No!'

When I decided to embark on a UK theatre tour of my talk show *An Audience with Noddy Holder* in the spring of 2013, I realized I was going to have to come up with a way of explaining the reasons behind that 'No!', even if it meant the downside of washing some of Slade's dirty laundry in public.

Part of the show would involve a question-and-answer session with the audience, so you didn't have to be Brain of Britain to figure out what one of the most popular questions would be!

My mate, radio and TV presenter Mark Radcliffe, was the host of the show. I've worked with Mark on and off for over twenty years and he was the perfect foil for me. He knows enough about me and my life to ask great questions and keep the stories and anecdotes flowing and he's not afraid to take the piss out of me either. I love that – I'd be there telling a tale about Freddie Mercury or Ozzy Osbourne and he'd make the audience laugh even more by ribbing me about the voices I was putting on. He reckoned my impressions were leaving a lot to be desired! Cheeky git. Though he was probably right.

I got my own back on him though. The stage set for the tour included an enormous golden throne for me to sit on, while Mark was provided with a rickety old kitchen chair. Occasionally during the show I'd let him have a little try and rest his backside on my padded rock-star throne, but it just didn't suit him. I'd tell him, 'You really don't have the necessary panache to carry that off', and he'd have to agree with me. He'd tell the audience I was too flash and it was one of my dining-room chairs. Harsh but true.

Mark and I cemented our friendship when I was a regular contributor to his BBC Radio 2 evening show.

We'd spend hugely entertaining evenings exploring all sorts of subjects on air – oh, and playing some music along the way. We were never afraid of heading off on some bizarre tangent, which is the way radio works best. Mark and his co-presenter Stuart Maconie, who joined the show in later years, were brilliant at tapping into their incredible knowledge of all sorts of subjects to create an entertaining radio show about the weirdest stuff.

I was officially booked as the TV reviewer. When at home I am a TV addict, a habit picked up as a result of killing time watching shows in hotel rooms when I was touring with the band all around the world (only when there was a lack of company, of course). Often, I wouldn't have a clue what on earth was going on in some dodgy Spanish soap opera or a crazy game show in Japanese. Alice Cooper told me he has a TV set turned on in every room of his house 24/7 – he obviously has the same affliction as me.

Aside from TV reviewing Mark would get me involved in discussions prompted by listeners' phone calls or emails. We could wind up talking about anything from musical tastes to how many pairs of shoes one man should own (more of that later …). My particular favourite was one that came up every year, on annual National Cheese Day.

National Cheese Day may not be as universally recognized as Christmas or Easter, but it got us very excited on the Radcliffe and Maconie show. It's funny how talking about cheese on toast over the airwaves can get people's gastronomic juices flowing enough to phone or email in their droves. We would get all sorts of wild and wonderful ideas on what makes this humble delicacy so appetizing...Does the bubbling cheese rest between two slices of toasted bread or rest on top of the two slices? Do you toast both sides of the bread or just the outside around the cheese? Do you butter the bread or not? Do you add Worcestershire Sauce or pickle while grilling or at the end? We had dozens of extra fillings suggested. Onion and/or tomato, of course, but also chilli, apple, marmite...sardines...*What*? There were even suggestions of fruitcake, jam and chocolate. People's tastes...wowie zowie!

We could have done a two-hour show just on the personal preferences of this common, simple snack. We would even cook some suggestions on air as a taste test...ah, the beauty of radio...

Anyway, I digress, as I will be apt to do during this book – a habit of mine, I'm afraid.

Mr Radcliffe had badgered me for years to go out on the road and recreate, for the benefit of audiences at intimate theatre venues, the sort of discussions we've had in many pub sessions.

In 2013 I finally agreed. The timing was perfect as it was the anniversary of my fiftieth year in showbiz and sixty years since I first got up on stage singing in working men's clubs in the industrial Black Country of England, aged seven. (Yes, folks, I'm *that* old. I know I don't look it but I put that down to the pure and clean life I've led.)

The basic idea for the evening's entertainment was to follow my life story from my baby-boomer birth in 1946 to the present day via conversation, anecdotes and film clips. A surprise for the audience was that I also had a guitar on stage and threw in some acoustic songs for good measure.

The show was not intended to be exactly the same every night and we could veer off in any direction at any time, which suited me down to the ground. This was helped along greatly during the second half of the show, when we would include the question-and-answer section with the audience. Some of the questions would come from cards put in a box strategically placed in the theatre bar before the show. Mark would sift through these in the interval and try and catch me unawares with some of them on stage. Other questions came direct from the crowd during the show, although some nights it could get hilariously out of hand and Mark would have to rein things in. This was all part of the fun. One of our favourite questions came on the first night of the tour and we ended up keeping it in most nights as it always got a laugh. It was:

'Suzi Quatro...Did ya?'

It was always a backstage bet as to how long it would take for someone to ask:

'Will you ever get back with Slade?'

I think the record was ten seconds. I decided it wouldn't be fair just to answer with 'It's not going to happen', without any qualification. I confronted the inevitable question head on. On stage every night Mark made the point that I usually got the blame for the break-up of the band, which I guess is largely true.

To cut a very long story short(ish). At the end of 1983 Slade had done a British tour to go alongside our big hit record, 'My Oh My'. Although the tour was successful, things were not so harmonious behind the scenes. Cracks in the band had started to appear.

The next year we went on tour to America because a cover version of one of our old hit songs, 'Cum on Feel the Noize', by a band called Quiet Riot, was topping the charts over there. Also, our current European hit 'Run Runaway' was charting in the US partly due to the video for the song being played on heavy rotation on the new and very important MTV video channel. However, the American tour was unexpectedly curtailed due to one of the band contracting hepatitis. So after a couple of weeks of doing promotion on the West Coast, we duly returned to the UK.

On getting home I found that my wife Leandra was going to be filing for divorce. This was a bolt out of the blue. We'd been together for ten years and I think she'd had enough of my lifestyle and we'd just been growing apart. The thing was, we also had two young daughters to consider and I needed to be around to help and soften the blow. I knew that those sorts of traumas in kids' lives can be devastating and I wanted it to be handled in the best way possible.

On top of all that, my father had been taken very ill and my mother needed me to be on hand in the UK to help them through this tough time.

So I had major issues to contend with in my personal life and the truth is that Slade were not gelling as we had done in the sixties and seventies. It used to be the four of us against the world, but since our career revival in the early eighties personality clashes were beginning to pull us apart.

I suppose it's understandable that when four guys have been working together pretty much day in, day out for nearly twenty years, complications will raise their ugly heads. In any rock group these issues tend to involve egos, money, women, drink and drugs, and, of course, the perennial 'musical differences'. Yes, and sometimes all of the above. There's a reason *This is Spinal Tap* is a film which all musicians love. The mock documentary, or 'rockumentary' if you like, about a British heavy metal act has got every rock 'n' roll cliché covered and I love the film's epitaph that reads 'It does for rock 'n' roll music what *The Sound of Music* did for hills'...genius. The scenes where they are all falling out about ridiculous stuff are spot on and hilarious, but it's not so much fun when it happens for real.

Due to what was happening at home, I told the band I was not going on the road for the foreseeable future. I offered to step down and they could replace me if that's what they wanted. Both a UK and a European tour had been booked in, but I had never agreed or signed up to do either. I don't break contracts.

I simply felt I had to make the family my priority. I thought if I could sort out my personal life and concentrate on that, it would also give the band breathing space from one another. Life on tour is very intense and all-consuming. I figured that if we just got together to write and record, things could possibly settle down and get back to normal...whatever qualifies as 'normal' in a rock 'n' roll band like Slade.

One ego in a band is to be expected and can be coped with; two egos are manageable; but trying to be democratic when you've got four egos pulling in different directions, then something has to snap.

It's well known in the music industry that many groups carry on working together for financial reward even though they don't get on with one another at all.

They travel separately, stay in different hotels, have their own dressing rooms and only ever really see one another when they get on stage. Sorry, but that would not be for me. I liked the shared camaraderie of the band and road crew having fun altogether on tour. What made Slade special was that the teamwork was real. We were at our best when we were working together and all heading in the same direction off stage as well as on. That was the magic of Slade: four pieces of a jigsaw fitting together perfectly.

Unfortunately, since the original line up broke up back in 1991 relationships between the members of the band have still not improved. So much for my theory that we all just needed some 'space'.

A few years ago I decided to get all the original Slade members together for a couple of meetings so that every-one could air their grievances face to face for a change. At the back of my mind was the thought that it would be worth seeing if there was any spark left and the slightest chance we could get back on stage together for one last tour. For my own peace of mind, I wanted to be sure.

The meetings were not an experience I want to repeat by any stretch of the imagination. It was like being back in the school playground, going over things that had allegedly been said over the years, much of which I knew nothing about. It was all: 'So and so said this …' and 'Somebody else said that …'

The contents of interviews printed in magazines and newspapers were brought up and raked over. Those sorts of articles – and certainly the headlines and captions the editors choose to use – were totally out of our hands and inaccuracies and misquotes were commonplace. After fifty years in the game you would think all the band members would have got used to all that stupidity.

It shouldn't really matter what some old article said anyway. The four original members of the band should know the truth. At the meetings all those external interferences were being given priority over the twenty-five years the band had worked together through all our highs and lows. It was as though all the respect for what we had been through and achieved was gone. Along with the trust.

I knew when I walked away from those meetings that I had done the right thing when I left Slade all those years before. Although I loved the guys and would always be proud of what we'd achieved, I could not have envisaged spending another six months together, let alone another twenty-five years. It would have been like four bad marriages all carrying on at the same time.

So the answer to the question 'Will you ever get back with Slade?' is still a resounding 'No!'

There are many more important things to do than to be arguing over a life I left behind twenty-odd years ago. The fellas really don't know what my life has been like since the early nineties, just as I don't really know what theirs have been like.

It was a pity and a regret because it would have been nice for us all to sit down for meals together and have a laugh about some of the outrageous things that happened in our misspent 'youth'. Maybe I'll put it down to us all being grumpy old farts. It makes it funnier and easier to accept.

Whatever other people think of me is really none of my business.

Today I look back at my days with Slade with huge satisfaction and pride in all that we achieved. We were just four lads from the Black Country who were catapulted to fame at a time when being top of the charts meant you'd sold literally millions of records. Our energy and enthusiasm were so infectious it was less a case of us not knowing what had hit us than the rest of the world not knowing what had hit them.

It still makes me laugh to see footage of us on old recordings of *Top of the Pops*, with Dave Hill dressed as an overstuffed cockerel, shedding feathers all over the stage, in the suit we used to call 'Foghorn Leghorn' (I say, I say!) after the cartoon character. Not forgetting as well what we called his 'Metal Nun' outfit – how could anyone forget the black habit topped off by a glittering silver wimple?

He famously would always get changed for TV appearances in the dressing-room toilet. This was so we couldn't see what bizarre design was coming next until he had donned the complete ensemble. Can you imagine it? Dave banging and crashing about inside the toilet trying to shoehorn himself into his latest skin-tight, space-age, jewel-encrusted creation, complete with matching platforms, shoulder pads and headdress! Such was the anticipation at the sound of him using cans of hairspray to attach glitter to various body parts.

All would suddenly go quiet and we would know he was finally ready. It was always the same ritual. I'd shout out, 'C'mon, H [his nickname in the band]. Reeeeveaaal ...' Eventually he'd appear, red-faced but delighted with his new 'look' like a sparkly Martian on acid. We'd all just piss ourselves laughing, but he didn't care. Jim Lea, the 'serious' member of the band, would have his head in his hands and say, 'I'm not going on television with you dressed like that.'

Dave's classic reply: 'You write 'em, I'll sell 'em!'

He knew the audience would love it and he was right. It was an unbelievable sight looking out from the stage into the crowd to see a multitude of mirrored top hats, like my own trademark hat, and all those glittering colourful costumes. Slade nights were outrageous, noisy and totally over-the-top.

We might have looked like a load of nutcases on stage but the fact was that throughout the biggest years of our success we were still just four Black Country lads let loose on the world. I'm sure part of our mass appeal was that our fans recognized that we never fell into the trap of trying to be cool. We wouldn't have had a clue anyway.

Our first trip to America in 1972 was a case in point. We arrived in the blazing sunshine of LA with palm trees and huge flashy American cars everywhere we looked. It was like being in a movie and certainly didn't look anything like Wolverhampton or Walsall.

The record company had organized for two stretch black limousines, which were parked outside the airport doors, to collect us and drive us in style to our hotel on Sunset Strip. Trouble was, no one had thought to tell us.

Not believing that these huge limos could be for us, we spotted this big minibus that was being loaded with all our luggage. Thinking this was our transport, in we jumped and, eager to get into the city, we said to the driver, 'Let's go, go, go.' The Polydor Records people only realized what was happening when it was too late and started shouting and madly waving their arms at us. We were just chuffed to be in LA so we grinned and waved back.

The roadies had a high old time travelling in *our* limos, cruising past us while we were cramped in the minibus and showing us their bare arses through the windows. So much for our rock-star arrival in the good ol' US of A!

We certainly knew how to play the rock star where it mattered most, though – on stage!

A Slade show was an event. We wanted to make the band and audience as one, with no mental barrier between us. We were one of the loudest bands on the planet and for twenty years doing gigs all over the world, we always gave 100 per cent on stage. The atmosphere was pandemonium and even all these years on people come up to me and tell me about when they saw us live. They remember the shows vividly – the music, the costumes, the lights, the between-songs patter, the audience participation and, importantly, how they felt when they got home. It was an experience and something that has stayed with them, and still makes them smile when they remember that special night. I can't ask for any more than that: it's what matters to me and how I want to remember those days.

I did the best I could and everything else is everybody else's problem.

In the early eighties a big-time American music mogul came over to me in a London hotel bar after hearing a radio show where Slade had been interviewed. This guy had handled some hugely successful US artists in his time. He took me to one side and in a no-nonsense, straight-talking Brooklyn accent said: 'You guys are over as a band, you know. You've now become a group.'

I thought this was a very strange thing to say and asked him what on earth he meant. 'One of your guys, all through the radio interview, was saying "I did this" and "I did that". I've seen this so many times with musicians and it's the first sign that all is not sweet apple pie in the ranks when "we" is constantly replaced by "I".'

I laughed at the time and said: 'I think you're reading something far too deeply into that interview.'

He came back with: 'Just you wait and see...and remember who told you.'

The guy didn't look much like a prophet, but his experience of the entertainment world had made him wise to the ways of musicians. Over the next few months his words started to make sense.

There is no 'I' in team, or so the cliché goes. Well, I know my spelling has been a bit peculiar over the years, but there is certainly no 'I' in band.

As the slow breakdown of the band and my marriage all happened around the same time, I had no real idea what the future held in store. With Slade there was never a clear-cut decision that we'd made our last record or performed our last gig. The door was always left open – who was to know what could happen down the line? We had been in the same sort of situation back in 1980 when the band had pretty much split up. Out of the blue came an offer to do the Reading Rock Festival in the summer. We stole the festival, took the headlines on the front pages of the music papers, got another major record deal and our new material began getting played on radio.

My life now, however, was taking on a whole new direction as I stepped away from touring and came to terms with my divorce. As anyone who has been through a divorce knows, it's an incredibly upsetting and difficult time. There are many things to take into account on top of the stress: all the practical stuff such as who has the kids and when, who lives where, how to divide up the money and possessions and, of course, all the legal dilemmas.

Once you bring in the lawyers things certainly don't get any simpler.

In my case my ex-wife wanted to move back to Manchester to be nearer her family, so I had to finance a house for her. I didn't want to sell the family home in the Midlands, if I could help it. It was too big for just me but I thought it would help the transition for the kids if every other weekend, when I brought them down from Manchester, they were living in their old family home. I was feeling guilty for the upheaval.

My divorce was an amicable affair compared to most, but even so, overnight my assets were cut in half. I now had to deal with alimony payments and child support. The everyday running costs of my own life were still the same and I still had to make sure my taxes were paid on time. Taxmen are not sympathetic to your personal situation, that's for sure.

Don't get me started on income tax! After paying eighty-three pence in the pound in the seventies I think I've put my fair share into the country's coffers over the years. I could have upped sticks and left the UK and been much better off financially – many others did. We as the band decided to stay residents of the UK and pay over the top for the privilege. If that's not being loyal to your country, I don't know what is.

Taxman, he say: 'seventeen pence for you, eighty-three for me!'

Yes, you took your pint of blood, Mr Taxman, and it was very nearly an armful! To top it all you pissed much of it up the wall.

Although a socialist at heart I've never forgiven that Labour government for ripping us off and driving many other big earners out of the country. I haven't got any problem at all with paying a decent amount of tax, but the rate was beyond ludicrous. The whole policy totally defeated the object because they got naught from those people at the end of the day. Not only did they drive away some of the biggest taxpayers but it meant some of the most talented and creative people in the country went to live elsewhere. This then had a knock-on effect of how many British people would be employed by these tax exiles. What a ridiculous way to run a country.

I also had to make changes to another money matter around this time. During the early eighties the band had been breaking even touring due to the two songwriters in the band, me being one, propping up the Slade touring expenses from our writing royalties.

That now had to stop as my income was needed elsewhere.

At this time Slade were still writing and recording and doing promotion all over Europe but our record sales, although very good, were not what they had been in the early seventies. It was a tricky time.

All this, of course, was nothing compared to me having to get used to my new domestic set up. I was of ye olde school in those days, when most men didn't handle the household chores. I had to learn how to do my own laundry for a start, but first I had to find where the hell the bloody washing machine and dryer were situated.

'Where is that darned washing machine, and where's the bloody manual to tell me how to work it?'

I had to start shopping for food stuffs and everyday household goods like toilet rolls and washing powder. Don't laugh – this is something that most men didn't have to deal with in those days. Especially me. I'd spent a big chunk of my life away touring all over the world. These domestic trivialities didn't occur on the road.

My wife had done all that stuff at home and on the road dirty clothes went to the hotel laundry. You ordered up room service for everything else you needed. Oh, how pampered we pop stars were. Mind you, we were paying for it all.

I had to eat so I needed to learn how to cook as I had no desire to live in restaurants or survive solely on takeaways. In the past I could muster a decent cooked breakfast or a bowl of soup, but that was about it.

There was nowhere near the amount of cookery items on TV then as there is today. Now, you can learn how to be a Domestic Goddess with Nigella, do Mom's Hockey Puck Meatloaf with the Hairy Bikers or be a Naked Chef with Jamie Oliver. I have tried cooking just in my apron but that hot oil does tend to get everywhere.

But back then, one of the only cooking shows on TV was *One is Fun!* with Delia Smith. (One can be fun, Delia, if you know what I mean, but to be honest I'm more of a party animal by nature.) It seemed the perfect place to start, so I videoed every episode and then went out and bought the accompanying book to the series. It set me off on a love of cooking that became a great hobby for me – very therapeutic and pleasurable. (Thanks, Delia...for everything!)

If I start on something I like to do it properly and well, and with cooking you never stop learning. I drive my wife Suzan mad because every time I've been out browsing the charity shops I always come back with at least one cookery book that someone else has discarded, often brand new. Our kitchen is full of them, from Elizabeth David to the *Sopranos Family Cookbook* to *Cook Yourself Thin (How to Drop a Dress Size)*. That last one has no worn pages so far.

I've never mastered ironing clothes properly, though. That's what I tell the wife anyway. She's pretty good at it... not the *only* thing she's good at, I may say, and that, dear reader, is why I married her!

All of this enforced domesticity was a total life change for me but over the next couple of years I adapted well considering the sort of life I'd been leading up to then. Well, you have to. There was no way I was going to sit at home alone drinking myself into a stupor every day. I can still drink with the best of them, but I've always been a social drinker. I love going to a bar with mates but I've never been one to drink at home unless we have guests round.

At this time I was considering moving out of the UK to live for a while. I thought a spell in Paris or New York, two cities I love a lot, might recharge me personally and artistically. New York would have been too far to go when my daughters were younger, but I could easily imagine making a new life for myself in Paris. Days spent at pavement cafés watching the world go by and scribbling thoughts, ideas and song lyrics in my notebook was a romantic and appealing plan. I already knew some of the local lingo anyway: '*Voulez-vous coucher avec moi, ce soir?*' Well, it's only polite to know the basics, isn't it?

It's never been a problem for me, settling in a new city. I have lived in a few different countries in my time and I can subscribe to the adage, 'Wherever I lay my hat, that's my home'. You have to be able to live like that anyway when you tour the world with a band. You're never in one place for that long.

I always remember one of my dad's sayings: 'You only need one meal a day, one pair of shoes and a roof over your head. Everything else is a bonus'.

I think he'd come to this conclusion after he'd spent six years fighting overseas in the Second World War. After that everything must have seemed like a bonus.

My parents were great for giving me a solid foundation for my life. They had no airs and graces and weren't that impressed with material wealth. They knew the value of family and being there for each other. They were just as delighted with a letter I'd send them from somewhere like Tokyo than any fancy presents. So long as I kept in touch and saw them as much as I could, then they were happy.

When I first made some real money I tried to buy my parents a nice house in the Midlands. They wouldn't move, wanting to stay where they were comfortable and be near their friends. Their house wasn't big but it was cosy and full of all their memories.

My dad said: 'Son, you might need that money some-day. We've already got all we want.'

They were really happy with their lot and there is a lesson to be learned from that in modern-day society. The main goal in life, surely, is to be totally happy. It has nothing to do with wealth. It does help if you have your health.

I have met a lot of extremely wealthy people over the years and I've come to realize very few of them are totally happy. Perhaps it's because there is always someone with more money than they have or some latest thing they don't yet own.

My mum and dad knew it, and I came to learn it too: with money and success there is always a price to pay.

When my time with Slade came to an end, I had no idea of what would happen next. I'd had the belief that I'd been in the best band in the world: how do you fol-low that? The last thing I wanted to do was make music at that time. I wanted a break from it and I could sense that things were changing in the business. The feeling I had when I first experienced the sound of Little Richard in 1957 had nothing to do with the current industry, so I exited stage right before it was too late. Many people reach a crossroads in their careers but it can be difficult to cope with in the glare of publicity.

I always knew there would be another route to happiness. The only question would be: which path would I take?

I see the positive in most situations and know that even something that at first looks like a setback is often just an opportunity in disguise. So life after Slade became an opportunity to explore lots of other career possibilities – radio and TV presenting, voiceovers and adverts, acting and writing. I wouldn't have been able to do any of those things easily if I'd stayed with the band. For more than fifty years I've been a professional 'artiste' – that really is what it's always said on my passport! It's unusual to be able to maintain a career in the industry for that long but I think the fact I've been able to adapt and do a variety of things has helped.

I get quizzed a lot about how much money you can make in showbiz, but when people ask me if I'm rich, I'll say: 'Compared to who?'

Compared to Paul McCartney, the answer would be: 'No'.

Compared to my mum and dad, I'd have to say: 'Yes'. They weren't rich moneywise, but they were mega rich as human beings.

Chapter Two

ANY WAY THAT YOU WANT ME

Sorry to disappoint you but these days I don't actually dress in gaudy seventies-style flared trousers and platform shoes. I never wear my top hat with mirrors on a night out and I only ever bellow 'It's Christmaaaaasssss' if I'm being paid a decent amount of money by an advertising company to do so. Perhaps I make an exception in the throes of passion, should the mood take me.

At Christmastime I don't go round to every pub, restaurant and shopping centre to insist they play Slade's 'Merry Xmas Everybody' on a loop until you are all driven to distraction. Nor did I also write 'I Wish It Could Be Christmas Everyday' by Wizzard, 'Merry Christmas Everyone' by Shakin' Stevens or Elton's 'Step into Christmas'.

You may think this needs no clarification, but I've spent hour upon hour in bars fending off tipsy folk who insist on crediting me with recording every Christmas hit ever released, along with pretty much the entire chart rundown of the early 1970s. One memorable night recently I was trapped in a bar by a drunken rugby team who accused me of singing on records by Sweet, Mud, Wizzard, Queen, Black Sabbath and T-Rex. They never went as far as confusing me with Suzi Quatro, but they never actually mentioned Slade either.

I heartily agreed with each of them in turn as the players sang, at the top of their voices, 'Ballroom Blitz' (by Sweet, incidentally), 'Tiger Feet' (yes, by Mud) and 'I Wish It Could Be Christmas Everyday' (*that* one's by Wizzard…that man with the funny make-up and the funny hairstyle. Okay, yes, I know I've got a funny hair-style as well, but it's not me!). My mates were pissing themselves as I was saying, 'Ah yes, that was one of the best ones I ever did' to every song. There must be people who to this day proudly boast how the Crown Plaza Hotel Bar in Birmingham that night had present the vocalist on almost every seventies glam rock classic.

The attention I do get when I'm out and about is 99 per cent complimentary. It's nice to be thanked all the time for giving people great memories. Just occasion-ally, though, you'll come across someone who can't resist having a little dig. I think it's probably because people sometimes don't know what to say when they come face to face with me in the flesh, but feel an overwhelming urge to say something. Their fallback position is to produce an insult. I don't let it bother me too much. Drives my missus nuts, though.

I never mind people coming up and shaking my hand or wanting to take a photo on their mobile phone. The trouble is no one, I repeat, *no one* ever has their phone camera ready to go. It's at the bottom of their handbag, it's not charged or the flash doesn't go off. They'll give it to someone else to take the shot who hasn't got a clue how that particular phone works. Then there's ten easy ways to chop off a head. 'Oh no, I don't like how I look on that one. Can we just do one more?' and then one more, and one more. 'I've set it to video ...', 'Damn, that one is all blurry', 'I can't send that to my Aunty Hilda/ put that on Facebook/tweet it to the waiting world!' Smartphones, my arse. 'Noddy, can I bother you for just a second?'... Ten minutes later your face is still fixed in a manic grin that will immediately be plastered over social media from here to China. Next thing you know you've drawn a crowd because they're curious as to what's going on. So then they also want pictures, and by the time you're finished you've missed your train.

Once on the train, however, another problem can occur. Mobile phones with built-in cameras mean every person is potential paparazzi. You can spot them a mile off, walking up and down the carriage, phone non-chalantly in hand. As they draw level they whip it up and 'click'...a blurry photo of Noddy sipping his tea or blowing his nose or catching forty winks after a heavy day. Minutes later the image is proudly displayed on Facebook or Twitter. I don't agree with David Cameron on much, but didn't he once say, 'Too many tweets make a twat'? When it's an invasion of my privacy and without my permission, I do have to agree.

It is thirty years since the must-have yuppie accessory, the mobile phone, was first launched. In 1984 it weighed 12 lb and had to be carried over the shoulder with a battery pack. Originally it was designed for doctors, vets, journalists and sales reps, people on the move. Now people can't even go to the toilet without taking their mobile with them. It's weird that the title of George Orwell's futuristic book, *1984*, with 'Big Brother is watching you' as the theme, should coincide with the launch of a device that now nearly everyone uses to watch one another.

I try to give the public what they want as best I can. I will pose for photos in most circumstances. I do draw the line at the gentlemen's urinal, though – chancers have tried to get a shot of my manhood a few times. I'm not the shy type and happy with my bits and pieces, but if I'd wanted them photographed I'd have become a porn star.

It's also awkward when you get up for a dance if you are at a 'do'. I like a boogie with the best of them and fancy myself as a bit of a nifty mover. Suddenly there's a sea of camera phones pointing in your direction. It was a shock when it happened the first time because you'd rather not have your 'dad dancing' posted all over the place, but I suppose it comes with the territory these days.

Another situation that's a no-no is when I'm at a restaurant in the middle of a meal with family or friends. Some people can't wait until I've finished eating and haven't got a mouthful of spaghetti carbonara before they venture over. I was once out with my mate, radio presenter Geoff Lloyd, when a bloke came up to me in the restaurant just as we're tucking in and opened with 'I don't like to bother you, Noddy ...' I couldn't resist saying, quick as a flash, 'Well, why are you then?' Geoff almost choked. He says it was the only time he has seen me refuse to sign an autograph. I did sign willingly afterwards but sometimes I get abuse for not signing right away, so then I will just blank the aggressor.

The folk I don't understand are the ones who clearly think I should be the same age, and look the same, as if I have just stepped off the *Top of the Pops* set circa 1973. Young TV researchers can be the worst for that. It's not their fault – they weren't even a twinkle in their parents' eye in those days. They've obviously Googled me and have an image in their head from clips they've found on YouTube.

It's been said many times that I've grown into my looks. It might be a back-handed compliment but I'll take it. I think what they mean is the fact that I was never a pretty-boy pop star, and more like a character from a Dickens novel, has now worked in my favour. The downside of that can be that people get a shock when it dawns on them how old I really am. I reckon it's the only reasonable explanation for some of the more extreme reality TV offers I regularly get.

The regular shows such as *Big Brother*, *I'm a Celebrity ... Get Me Out of Here!* and *Strictly Come Dancing* all ask me to do their show pretty much every year. They are just the tip of the iceberg, though ... literally. Do you remember an ITV show called *71 Degrees North*? Ten celebrities were taken to the Arctic and asked to complete challenges like jumping into a pool of frozen water, staying in for sixty seconds before climbing out, stripping down to their underwear and then running through the deep snow to the finish line. The fastest contestant would be immune from the vote off. You don't say! There was more ... a team of celebrities had to dive off a boat into a lake and then swim to shore. Once on shore they made their way to a cliff where they abseiled facedown before, yes, you guessed it, racing for the finish line. Now, flattering though it was to be asked, I'm a pensioner, for heaven's sake! Last year I went arse over tit on my way to post a letter in the village when there was a light snowfall ... By the way I've said no to *Dancing on Ice* too. Me in Lycra ... not a pretty sight.

We play a game in my house when these offers come through on email. It's called 'Let's Spot the Un-real Reality

TV Show'. Sometimes spoof invitations are sent out by journalists pretending to be TV companies. It's a ruse to find out how desperate some celebs are to appear on TV. They come up with the most ridiculous, over-the-top idea for a show, and then write an article in a newspaper with the names of the famous people who have agreed to do it, and for how much money. The task is to spot the fakes.

Over the last few years I've been invited to take part in *Celebrity Shark Bait*, where you are plunged into shark-infested waters with just a metal cage between you and a shiver of man-eating sharks. *Back to Mine*, a programme about celebrity potholing involving crawling into caves or abandoned mines deep underground and generally wriggling about in mud for days. Both of these were for real. There was *CelebAir*, where for no good reason I could become a flight attendant on an aeroplane taking people on their hols. We were convinced that one was a hoax. The email invitation even came from a researcher calling himself Del Conboy...Guess what? That one was real too and so was he, although it was cancelled after one series due to poor ratings and low celebrity interest.

The one I quite fancied was *Celebrity Detox Camp*, a Channel 5 show where the likes of Richard Blackwood, Keith Duffy and Tamara Beckwith (she took part in *CelebAir* too; are you sensing a pattern?) were flown to Thailand for a fortnight of intense detoxification, fasting, exercise and rigorous massages. Mm, a fortnight in

Thailand, you say? Emerging fitter, slimmer and health-ier, with massages on the beach given by dusky maidens? Tempting…until I got to the part about the colonic irrigation, with self-administered coffee enemas several times *every day*. They were kind enough to provide you with your very own length of hose to insert where the sun don't shine, with a bowl to catch the matter washed out in the process. The contents of your bowels would then be held aloft for all to see, the whole thing filmed in all its stomach-churning detail. Although my missus thinks I have a pert bottom, to put it on display in these circumstances, I think not. Kim Wilde was the only one who stuck to the regime and won the show. Good for you, gal, but it's not for me.

I always turn down TV offers that want to hone in on your personal life. I've never done a TV or photo shoot in my own home and even though the cash offers can be substantial, I never will. I even turn down those 'What's in Your Fridge?'-type magazine features.

The exception to the rule was when I agreed to go on ITV's *All Star Mr and Mrs* in 2010 with my wife Suzan. The prize money you can win for charity was the big draw for me – a jackpot of £30,000.

We had started dating in 1990, just over twenty years earlier, after meeting on a late-night TV debate show in Birmingham called *Central Weekend Live* (Suzan worked on the show). I reckoned we knew each other pretty well and we'd played the *Mr and Mrs* board game with friends, so I was fairly confident we wouldn't disgrace ourselves. Suzan wasn't so sure. Even after years of working in television production she's not that confident in front of the camera. Generally speaking she is more than happy to let me hog all the limelight, but on this show there was nowhere to hide. It is called *Mr AND MRS* after all.

Before the show Suzan was nervous, *very* nervous. It didn't help that I was merrily chatting to all and sundry with not a care in the world. In the make-up room we got to say a quick hello to the other couples taking part, who were also having an attack of nerves. Walking into the studio, Suzan seemed to calm down a bit as she was on familiar territory, so I thought she could take a joke. As we stood at the top of the stairs ready for our introduction, I looked at her and whispered, 'Right, I want to win this, okay?...And make sure you're funny!' With that I started off down the stairs towards Phillip Schofield and Fern Britton...Suzan made sure I paid for that later. Apparently that wasn't the best time to make a joke!

The questions were tricky – they don't make it easy for you at all – but we got all but one of them right. When they showed Suzan three pictures of me dressed in a variety of stage outfits and asked her to choose which one she preferred, she was forced into making an embarrassing confession.

One of the pictures was of me in a Santa suit, the outfit I would wear to end the stage show on December tours when we played the Christmas hit. For my wife it had made another appearance in a less public setting.

Suzan told Phil and Fern, and several million viewers, about the first Christmas we spent together when Santa made a personal appearance in our house.

She had to admit that she'd been a rather naughty girl that year. It was Christmas Eve and I told her I thought I'd heard a noise outside in the garden. I went to investigate. Meanwhile, in our bedroom, 'Santa' appeared, dressed in what appeared to be an identical suit to the one I used to wear on stage. He gave Suzan what she described on the show as . . . 'an extra surprise present'.

Mission completed, Santa disappeared and I returned to find Suzan somewhat flustered. She seemed to think I had something to do with the encounter. I've got no idea what she was talking about.

Luckily when I saw the pictures of the stage outfits on the TV show, I was certain she had chosen the Santa suit as her favourite.

Before we knew it, we were in the final. In that round it was my turn to go into the booth and be blindfolded and wear headphones. Suzan had to answer four questions: three on me and one about herself. It was at that point we almost came completely unstuck. The last question about me was a killer. Phillip asked her, 'Who was

Noddy's childhood crush?' Suzan said it was awful – she had not a clue at all what Phillip was getting at. She said she could not remember me mentioning any childhood crushes whatsoever, and I think she's right. I don't know where they got their information, but it certainly wasn't from me direct. The only idea she had was to say that I had been a huge fan of Al Jolson when I was young. Just in the nick of time she plucked a name from the air: the film star Bette Davis. I still love her films and her outspoken attitude to her life. Still, Suzan didn't have any hope that she had said the right answer.

When I came out of the booth I managed to match the first two answers straightaway. Then we got to the childhood crush moment. I was just as baffled as Suzan. 'Well,' I said. 'I did really like Al Jolson when I was a kid …?'

Phillip looked bemused. 'Would you say you had a *crush* on Al Jolson?' he asked.

Fair point. I thought hard, 'Well, I really don't know, I quite liked…Bette Davis?' I have no idea how we managed to match that answer; it was almost like we had some sort of telepathy going on. We must know each other even better than we thought we did.

That still left the jackpot question to answer. We'd won £15,000 so far and answering the next question could double that to £30,000, all for our chosen charity, the National Society for the Prevention of Cruelty to Children.

Phillip asked me, 'What was the name of the pro-gramme Suzan was working on when you met her?'

Was that it? Nothing like as tricky as the childhood-crush question, this one I knew. As soon as I said *Central Weekend Live* the audience cheered and fireworks went off in the studio. We'd done it, we won the jackpot. It was one of those big 'Yippee!' moments.

Once in a while I have got an offer for a TV role that's a bit like winning the jackpot in itself. Starring in the forti-eth anniversary live episode of *Coronation Street* was one of those. I'm a huge *Corrie* fan. I think it's a brilliant show – great writing, great acting, amazing characters and lots of comic touches amid all the drama.

It came about quite by chance. I was at an awards din-ner in Manchester in 2000 and seated at one of the big tables next to mine were a lot of the *Corrie* mob. I knew many of the cast through hanging out in Manchester and working at Granada Television, and they were telling me all about the planned upcoming live episode to celebrate the fortieth anniversary of the show. They knew I was a great fan and some of the actors started pestering the producers with 'Come on, let's get Noddy in the live ep. He's done some acting, it'll be great.' We were all having a great laugh and coming up with ridiculous suggestions of how to get me in it but I never took any real notice.

I thought it was all jolly pissed-talk. At that time there hadn't been any famous people making cameo appearances in *Corrie*.

Two days after the drunken dinner I got a message from the Granada top brass: they really did want to offer me a part in the live episode.

Now bear in mind this is the most watched show on TV five times a week, it's the fortieth anniversary and it's a completely *live* episode. I don't really get nervous, but this was out of my comfort zone. However, there was no way I was going to turn it down. Walking into that green room a few days later to see all those familiar faces from the cast was nerve-wracking, let me tell you.

I soon realized they were all terrified too. This was a huge deal and a real moment of TV history. They were determined to get it right.

Time was tight to put the whole thing together. Usually there's no rehearsal time on *Coronation Street* at all, the turnaround schedule is too fast. The main actors did have rehearsals for this though, but I had just one day to get my head around my lines, scenes cues and all the possible things that could go wrong in front of a TV audience of millions.

The cast could not have been nicer and more welcoming to me. I remember Anne Kirkbride, who plays Deirdre, being a real mother hen. She seemed to enjoy any downtime she had between scenes by putting on her rubber gloves and tidying the green room to make it as comfy as possible for everyone. As it was December she was trimming the place with Christmas decorations too. I don't know whether it was to calm the nerves but the rest of the cast didn't seem to bat an eyelid as she cleaned up around them.

My role was to be Stan Potter, a workmate of builder Duggie Ferguson, played by John Bowe. The storyline was that the council wanted to rip up the cobbles and tarmac Coronation Street: sacrilege. Stan and Duggie concocted a plot where they faked a preservation order to stop the diggers ripping up the street, and Stan arrived in the closing scenes of the show brandishing the piece of paper that saves the cobbles. Cue huge cheers from the street residents and a perfect opportunity for me to shout 'Merry Christmas Everybody!' before the closing credits.

Well, that was the plan. In rehearsal it looked like it could come unstuck. My final entrance was by black cab and I had just a minute to leap from the vehicle, say my lines and save the street. The timing was crucial, no chance for a second take. Every time we rehearsed the cab driver would be cued to drive in, I'd reach for the door handle ready to leap out, and the cabbie had locked the door. We tried the scene three times and every time it got to my bit I couldn't open the door of the bloody cab. In the end I practically got the poor cab driver by the throat. 'Look here, guv, if you lock this door tonight, I will actually strangle you live on air, do you understand?' He finally seemed to get the message.

John Bowe, being the professional he is, worked out a contingency plan that if the cabbie cocked up we would play the scene with me hanging out of the window. He had realized it would not be good form for me to commit murder live on television, although it would have guaranteed front-page news the next day. On the night my heart was hammering as the cab pulled up on the street. Thank God, the door opened and the scene went off without a hitch.

The weather was not on our side, though. There were lots of outdoor scenes and the wind and lashing rain were making the street action scenes very hard to shoot. The technical crews as well as hair, make-up and costume were battling the elements and miraculously keeping everything running smoothly. It turned out that the wind was a blessing in disguise. Some crazy idiot had planned to wreck the live episode by parachuting into the street during the broadcast, hoping to get himself on the news. Unfortunately for him the wind blew him way off course and he landed in a canal. Strange how things work out.

Actress Liz Dawn didn't have to worry about the weather. For all her scenes as Vera Duckworth she was in a hospital bed in a coma. Funnily enough, I remember she was just as nervous as the rest of us.

The inclusion of HRH Prince Charles in the episode was also giving all the cast and crew the jitters that day. He was visiting Granada to unveil a plaque commemorating the anniversary of the show. That's what he was supposed to be doing on the set, but the enterprising producers decided to film a sequence with him and Audrey Roberts (played by Sue Nicholls), who was then a Weatherfield local councillor. The footage appeared in the show as if Audrey was being presented to Prince Charles at Weatherfield Town Hall – a great idea.

It was a fantastic episode packed full of plot lines and fast-moving action from scene to scene, out on the cobbles, inside the Rovers, at Vera's hospital bedside and, despite all the nerves and the possibility of things veering out of control, it was a huge success. At the end of the hour-long show, as all the cast and crew were gathered in the street, the floor manager shouted at the top of his voice, 'IT'S A WRAP!' There was the most almighty cheer and such a sense of relief and pride that it had all gone so well. Just brilliant, and it's one of my proudest moments to have been a small part of an historic TV event.

Offers like *Corrie* don't come along every day. Many scripts I'm sent cast me as an ageing rock star, often to be found dead after an overdose of drink and drugs or floating face down in his own swimming pool by the end of scene two. I guess directors figure I lead a life of excess and debauchery and don't expect me to be able to be anything other than a wild rock 'n' roller. I can do that – I've had many years of practice to draw upon – but I like to think I have a few other strings to my bow.

I don't know whether it's because I'm a musician and/ or if it's to do with my Midlands accent, but I get the impression that a lot of people I meet expect me to be a bit thick and are surprised when I can string a coherent sentence together.

I get people commenting on the time I was on the TV show *Have I Got News for You* and gave my take on the world economy. Ian Hislop ended up saying, 'Noddy Holder should be in charge of the country's finances.' Quite right, I couldn't fuck it up any more than the bankers already have anyway.

It's the same when I appear on Matthew Wright's Channel 5 TV discussion show, *The Wright Stuff*. I watch the news and have a fairly decent grasp of current affairs so I don't find it too hard to give my take on the day's events and what's going on around the world.

Some folk may have very low expectations of me but I've been around a bit. I've seen a lot more of the world than most people and I listen and I learn. If I'm given a job to do I take it seriously. I don't just turn up and wing it. I research, prepare and like to think I know my craft, whether it's singing, writing, presenting, acting or doing voiceovers I always got right down to business with the band. No messing about, get it down, get it done quickly and get it done right. Even now, when I'm doing scenes or voiceovers. I'm known mostly as a one- or two-take wonder.

It's not a bad thing to surprise people and I usually get rebooked, which says something.

Find me a trend and I'll buck it!

Yes, you read it right first time. I've never been a follower; I prefer to be a leader. I cannot stand what I call the 'sheep' mentality, everyone following the rest of the herd.

Fashion is the obvious example where people can follow the pack instead of being an individual. There's nothing at all wrong with fashion itself, but I feel very strongly that a lot of people follow fashion slavishly and end up wearing things that really don't suit them. I'll never understand why so many women think Ugg boots look good. I don't get them at all. Keep Uggs for making your feet cosy indoors unless you want to go out shopping looking like a Yeti.

I always like to put my own spin on things and create looks from a combination of influences. Even at school kids used to take the piss out of me for what I wore and how long my hair was, and that was way back in the early sixties. You do need to have a certain kind of personality to be a little quirky, I know, and I'm not the slightest bit bothered about what people think of me. I certainly wouldn't let it change what I wanted to wear or what I wanted to do. Some people think I'm confident because I've reached a certain level of success and fame, but that's not it, I've always been the same.

As well as the mickey-taking I do get loads of compliments about the clothes I wear. I think you do have to have a certain panache to carry things off; you should never wear stuff or do things in an apologetic way. Be confident about it and you can get away with a lot.

I struggle to understand why so many bands today don't try harder with their image. They shuffle on to TV wearing a creased T-shirt and spend the whole performance singing to their shoes because they think it's cool. I prefer performers who really perform and can project charisma, if they have any, that is. Robbie Williams knows how to do it big style. Paloma Faith too – all that theatricality and costume as well as great music. I love all that.

Another pastime I have is hunting for treasures in charity shops or vintage stores, especially if I come across a favourite forgotten fifties vinyl LP (that's a long-playing twelve-inch plastic album to our younger readers). The iconic twelve-inch sleeves are as vital to me as the music.

I know most blokes hate shopping in all its forms, but not me. I love bookshops. I can spend hours poring over books about history, music, film, art and people; they all interest me. I've collected hundreds over the years – I just need to find time to read them all.

Find me a kitchen appliance store and I'm in heaven. As cooking is one of my hobbies, I've got a bit of a thing about kitchen gadgets. I'll watch somebody demonstrating a gadget and they make the tool look easy to use so I'll think to myself, that's just what I need. Always a mistake. When am I going to use that twirly thing to peel a pineapple or that special piece of rubber hose to get the skin off a clove of garlic? I've got a drawer full of this stuff. I tell myself to keep them as they'll be collectors' items one day. When will I ever learn?

I don't know what people might expect my home to be like, but I think visitors who come for the first time are a bit surprised by what they find. The décor is influenced by my interest in twentieth-century European history – mainly British, French and German.

I can't bear things being bland and nondescript. I like lots of colour, which is not surprising, I suppose. Each room in the house has a different style, ranging from art deco to art nouveau to Victoriana to 1940s/50s kitsch and things that are totally off-the-wall. I've collected some very strange things on my travels and there's something a bit unexpected everywhere you turn. It's bohemian, not to everyone's taste, and can be alarming if you're of a nervous disposition.

We once had a babysitter who refused to use the downstairs loo because she thought the lady mannequin head in there was looking at her in a funny way. If that doesn't get you there's an enormous Pinocchio puppet in there too, strung from the ceiling. He keeps a beady eye on your ablutions so we do have to warn some people. More often than not, we just wait for the scream when somebody enters.

My missus thinks I've gone too far with Lisa. That's the name of a four-foot high troll-like figure that came from a German 1920s fairground. She is pretty ugly but I think she has a certain charm. She's naked with enormous boobs, but Suzan really objects to her private parts, which are distinctly painted black. To show her off properly I've put her on top of a stack of speakers in the music room, so you get quite an eyeful as you enter. Suzan has tried to cover her modesty by draping a feather boa over her. I make sure she's not covered up for long, especially in the summer. The idea that these weird and wonderful inexpensive objects have survived and travelled from country to country, via different owners, and had a life of their own greatly appeals to me.

I'm the same with guitars. I have a few pre-owned vintage guitars, some very old. It's nice to know that they have been played at countless gigs and during their history have given pleasure to huge numbers of music lovers. These things in life have to be preserved for future generations. It's a risk when taking a beloved old instrument on a plane because any rapid change in pressure can cause the wood to crack and wreck the guitar. I store my collection in my old warehouse in the city and they take it in turns to come and visit me. I don't have them over more than one at a time because they get jealous of one another.

I had three guitars stolen during my time with Slade. All three were stolen by other so-called musicians. I use the term loosely because it is an unwritten law that you do not steal a fellow musician's instrument. I know who the culprits are and I'm sure they will get their comeuppance, and just maybe one day those guitars will find their way back home for a hug from Daddy.

As with décor and music, I think my taste in art is what you'd call eclectic. When you don't care what's trendy or the right thing to like, you can be free to enjoy whatever you want. I don't really get the whole Tracey Emin unmade bed or sheep-in-a-tank Damien Hirst sort of thing. I don't have a problem with those who do – art is, after all, in the eye of the beholder. I get off on the work of Salvador Dalí. Suzan and I spent hours in the Dalí museum in Montmartre, Paris, when we were on honeymoon. Toulouse-Lautrec and all the Parisian, Moulin Rouge era appeals to me, too, as do the German Expressionists.

*

Unlike some rock stars, comedians and celebrities, my public persona is pretty close to the real me, but my wife says I'm a strange mixture of Rocker and Domestic God. I'm house proud and can cook, clean and sew buttons on shirts. I'm more than happy to do the supermarket shop and whip up a meal but I am still equally at home partying into the wee small hours. I can take my booze and have never been drunk under the table by youngsters trying to get me sozzled. I've lost count of the nights I've spent in hotels where the bellboy has tapped me on the shoulder in the hotel bar to give me my wake-up call.

I am certainly not the greatest DIY expert in the world, but I do have a knack of being able to fix things. I do like a nice little repair job. On my recent talk tour, Mark Radcliffe asked what was in the small leather case I always have with me when I travel. I replied, 'It's my tool kit.' It drives me crazy that sometimes, even in the best hotel rooms, there will be something broken. A drawer that doesn't close properly, a wardrobe door or shower curtain hanging loose, a lamp that doesn't work. I can't be arsed to call down to housekeeping. No, I just get out my tool kit and fix it on the spot. When Mark found out about this he was amazed. I must be the only rock star who leaves a hotel room in a better condition than he found it.

Chapter Three

BABY BABY BABY . . . I LUV YOU

I was having lunch with the comedian Peter Kay when he came straight out and asked me an interesting question about coping with fame. We were in his trailer on location while filming his sitcom, *Max & Paddy*. I was guesting on the show, playing a car mechanic repairing their mobile home. I'd just removed the set of comedy buck teeth I wore as the character Mick Bustin, which was lucky because it was a pretty important question and I don't think Peter would have been able to have taken my considered response at all seriously if I'd still had those mangled gnashers in place. Peter does have a thing about comedy teeth and finds them most amusing.

Peter had made the leap from stand-up comedian on the club circuit to being Britain's best loved comedy star. His show *Phoenix Nights*, co-written with another great northwest comic, Dave Spikey, and set in the world of working men's clubs, had been a monster hit. *Max & Paddy* was the follow-up, featuring the adventures of the nightclub bouncer characters from that show, played by Peter and his Bolton school pal, Paddy McGuinness. Paddy has gone on to become a TV star in his own right.

Peter is a down-to-earth northern lad. He is incredibly talented as a writer, performer and a director and a lot of his popularity stems from his amazing ability to draw the audience's attention to the ridiculousness of everyday life. Whether it's how kids always slide around the floor on their knees at weddings, or the way the British talk about the weather, or the crazy things everyone's mother comes out with from time to time, he has a fantastic way of making ordinary life completely hilarious.

But ordinary life was exactly what he was starting to feel remote from. Along with the accolades and awards he was finding there was also a new emotion you have to deal with: the adulation.

There's no getting away from the fact that success in any form of show business brings a level of fame that you have to adjust to. Whether you get used to it is another matter – some certainly don't. I'll never understand the youngsters who cite 'fame' as an ambition. What do they want to be famous *for*? I wanted to be famous when I was a teenager, but famous for performing on stage, being given a recording contract and having hit records. They were all the motivating factors for me when I was starting out. I will admit that back in my teenage bedroom, strumming my guitar, I loved the idea of being fêted and well known. Back in those days, mind you, the cult of celebrity did not exist in the same way as it does now. You considered famous people to be big movie or music stars. You only ever saw them on huge cinema screens thirty-foot wide. Those people were larger than life, literally. You didn't get to see them in their pyjamas, putting out the bins. You didn't know every dot and comma of their lives. Even rock 'n' roll stars managed to retain a certain mystique to their private lives. There was no real scandal for Elvis when he took up with young Priscilla and moved her into Graceland when she was just sixteen. Can you imagine the furore there would be about that now? You never caught a glimpse of Little Richard unless he was made up, spruced up and with his Brylcreemed pompadour quiff in place.

The world is a very different, much smaller place today.

Even reality TV stars who have appeared in one series of a show such as *The Only Way is Essex* or *Geordie Shore* have their entire lives investigated and regurgitated for the entertainment of the masses. Their opinions on everything are asked and revealed; they are pictured in the supermarket, at the car wash, everywhere. With the eruption of technology there is no hiding place for 'celebrities'. Everyone has a mobile phone with a camera and they are not afraid to use it to expose every movement you make to the scrutiny of the world. It's like being under permanent surveillance.

The difficulty for an artist in this situation for the first time is to find a way to carry on as normally as possible under such intense attention. It can sometimes be very awkward but who wants to live in a gilded cage? For a comedian it is pretty essential to try and retain as much of a grip on normality as possible. How on earth can you tell a joke that will connect with people if you are disconnected with real life yourself?

For Peter, at that time, having such a high profile was still relatively new and I think he looked on me as a veteran of the business. Someone who'd managed to sustain a lasting career and was still recognizable, but who hadn't completely lost all his marbles in the process.

So he asked me, 'How have you handled it all for so many years? . . . What advice would you give someone like me? Is there anything you regret or would change?'

That's a big question and one I've been asked by many artists. The only important thing I could recommend was . . .

'Don't neglect your family.'

I went on to tell him that I don't have many regrets

in my life. I'm a positive person and I look on the bright side if at all possible. However, I do regret not spending enough time with my daughters when they were very young. Once you've missed those special moments there's nothing you can do about it.

When Charisse and Jessica were little, Slade were on a hectic work schedule and I could be away for months at a time. That's much too long for children. There was no Skype or such like in those days and the only link was your voice at the end of a phone. I remember coming home once and Jessie, who was no more than a baby, screamed the place down when I came towards her. She didn't know who I was.

My first wife Leandra was pretty much left to cope with all the nativity plays, concerts, sports days, parents' evenings and a lot of the day-to-day parenting on her own.

So I told Peter, 'The biggest mistake I made was missing out on a lot of my first two daughters growing up. Get the balance right. It's not easy but it's definitely something to watch out for.'

Working mothers with children have to face this dilemma every day. In any case, Peter takes his family life so seriously that he is well known in the business for returning home every night after work. No matter where he is gigging, he leaves the arena as the audience are still cheering, gets in his waiting car and drives home through the night to be at home with his wife Sue and his kids. He'll also organize his filming schedules to be as near to Bolton, his hometown, as possible.

In my defence I know there are lots of parents who are not away from home a lot but still don't manage to leave work to see their kids say, 'there's no room at the inn' or run the egg-and-spoon race. But when you are on a tour of Europe, for example, and you are due on stage in front of thousands, it really is impossible to pop back for a school play or a birthday party.

I've always had a brilliant relationship with my daughters and am lucky that they never held it against me. The kids understood what their daddy did as a job – it was what they were used to – but I do regret not seeing them more.

When I got another chance at fatherhood I was determined to do things differently.

Django was born in January 1995 when I was forty-nine years old. I never expected to be a dad again that late in life. Well, you don't, do you? When you are a young kid you think thirty is ancient.

I thought long and hard about whether it was the right thing to do. If I hadn't been the dad I wanted to be with my other children, was it wise to go into parenthood again being so much older? In the end I decided to go for it – without doubt one of my best decisions. It was fate, no matter what anybody else had to say.

Friends and family reaction to the news that Suzan was pregnant took us a little by surprise. Many of them made no effort to hide their reservations. My mum was so taken aback that she could hardly bring herself to admit to the fact we were having a baby, despite the sight of Suzan's bump getting larger and larger. Mum was one of those who believed that if you didn't have anything nice to say you were better off saying nothing at all. So she managed to ignore the situation for quite a while. It was only when my first wife, Leandra, reassured her that I had in no way been tricked or trapped into the pregnancy and the baby was totally planned that Mum at last started to relax, although she was worried about how I would cope with the demands of a young child at my age. For her generation it was hard to understand that I was becoming a dad when historically I was heading into grandfather territory. What bothered her too was the fact that Suzan and I weren't married at the time. Once the baby was born, however, she was completely besotted and he instantly became her 'little smasher'.

It wasn't the first time Suzan and I had come up against disapproval. There is a nineteen-year age difference between us and everyone had the opinion that our relationship was doomed from the off.

If they knew the real story of *how* we met and got together they probably would have given us even less chance of survival. It was definitely an unusual start.

As I've already revealed, I was appearing on the late-night debate show *Central Weekend Live* in Birmingham when our paths first crossed. Suzan was a researcher on that show and was tasked with looking after me and the other guests, briefing us about the topics and questions that might come up. She was chatty and friendly and we struck up a conversation about music and a trip she planned to take to Memphis and Nashville. She was twenty-four and I thought it was unusual that a lady of her age knew such a lot about fifties rock 'n' roll music and was serious enough to go and explore where it all began. I was attracted to her instantly as she had a cracking pair of legs. I have always been a legs and eyes man, and Suzan was loaded with qualities in both areas.

Other guests on the show that night included Joe Brown and Roy Wood, and Suzan took the opportunity to ask us to sign autographs ... for her dad! He's a big music fan and she wanted to give him a memento of the rockers she had met that night. She did make a point of telling us the first record she ever bought was Roy Wood and Wizzard's 'See My Baby Jive', so that put me firmly in my place. I remember saying to her, 'You don't really want my autograph for your dad, they all say that. It's for you, admit it! Mind you it's better than the "It's for my granddad" that I get sometimes these days.' She just laughed.

She made me laugh too and at some point in the evening I asked her if she was going for a drink after the show. Suzan, naive as she was, now says she thought I was simply asking was *everyone* going for a drink afterwards, not that I was particularly asking her. I'm not slow in coming forward with women but my irresistible charms were not working on Suzan, obviously. The Central TV studios were right next to the old Holiday Inn in Birmingham so at midnight, when the show finished, the production team, crew and guests all moved next door to have a drink, wind down and relax. Suzan says that when she entered the bar all she saw was me holding court and swapping dirty stories with a rowdy crowd of people surrounding me, so she never came anywhere near me. I hadn't seen her in the bar and everyone was getting fairly drunk. A little later on I went looking for her only to be told that she'd headed home. Charming. Ah well, you win some, you lose some, and that could well have been the end of that.

Just a week later I had to go into Central TV to do a voiceover for a documentary. Walking up the stairs I was almost knocked off my feet by a tornado dressed in a ridiculously oversized checked jacket, with legs sticking out below, ending in bovver boy-style Doc Martens. She was also wearing a black trilby pulled down over her eyes, but I recognized her straightaway. It was Suzan.

We chatted and I teased her, asking after her dad and if he liked the autographs. She was off on some job or other but before she disappeared again I asked if she fancied going out for a drink sometime. Again, Suzan says she still didn't register that I was asking her out. I'm not sure why my pulling powers were deserting me once more – I'd never had this sort of problem before. She casually said to call her at the office if I wanted and never gave me her home number (this was 1989, long before everyone had a mobile phone). Then she was gone in a blur of black and white check and stompy boots. Strange girl.

So I called her at her office, and I called again. I tried her several times over the next couple of weeks to no avail. Was she trying to tell me something? She'd failed to inform me that she was off for three weeks over the Christmas holidays.

When she got back to work she said she found all these messages on her desk, saying that a man had called repeatedly but wouldn't leave his name. She thought maybe it was a guest who hadn't been paid an appearance fee for the show and was ringing up to complain.

In early January I decided to give it one last go. This time Suzan answered and I asked if she fancied meeting me at the Holiday Inn bar for a drink one evening, after she finished work. It was at this point that she says the penny finally dropped. I was asking her out, yes, *on a real date*. She agreed, hesitantly, but as soon as she put the phone down apparently went into a bit of a meltdown. Why was I asking her out?...Was I married?...How old was I?...What did Noddy Holder want from her?...Why did I want to meet at the Holiday Inn, a hotel, with bedrooms!? *And me a rock star, with my reputation!* Well, maybe she had a point.

I was oblivious to the turmoil that I had created and I simply turned up at the bar at the agreed time. It was six o'clock in the evening and I'd been out filming all day. For Suzan it was not so straightforward. She'd got herself so worked up that she arrived at the bar a couple of minutes early and found I hadn't got there yet. Relieved, she ran back to the Central Weekend office as fast as she could. She was back at her desk at two minutes past the hour. I wasn't late so it didn't occur to me that I'd already missed her. She, however, was breathing a sigh of relief and had no intention whatsoever of giving me the benefit of the doubt and returning to see if I had arrived.

Then her boss got involved. Word had spread in the office that Suzan was meeting me that night. She'd only told one girlfriend but everyone had been talking about it behind her back. When producer Doug Carnegie saw her at her desk at the time he knew she should have been meeting me, he decided to act. He asked why she was still at work and she confessed she'd been to the bar but I hadn't been there. Doug said, 'Suzan, it's only five past the hour now, give the guy a break. He's the lead singer in one of Britain's biggest bands, he's a friend of this show and we might want to book him again in the future – you get yourself back round there this minute, and be nice!' Thanks, Doug...I think.

So she sullenly slunk back to the bar in a bit of a mood, saw me there waiting, strode up and the first words out of her mouth were, 'Well, you're lucky. I've been here once and you weren't here – I wasn't going to bother coming back!' I've had better greetings if I'm honest. Added to that rather fierce opener was the spectacle of what she was wearing. It wasn't quite what I was expecting, that's for sure.

To make certain that I did not get the wrong impression, and to underline the point that she was no twinky TV researcher that would hop into bed with the first lead singer in a rock band who clicked their fingers, she had dressed carefully for the occasion. Suzan style. She was wearing some ratty old jumper under a camouflage army jacket and tight black jeans tucked into those enormous Doc Martens of which she was clearly so fond. I also solemnly swear, m'lud, that she was wearing a balaclava. Suzan claims it was *not* a balaclava but a woollen 'snood'. But whatever you call it, it was a woolly concoction that covered her whole head except for the eyes. The whole ensemble did not add up to anything like what any woman had ever turned up wearing for a first date with me before.

Somewhat stunned by the whole turn of events I went to the bar to get us some drinks. I tried to work out how, hoping for a light romantic encounter on a cold, wet Monday night in Birmingham, I'd ended up with a snotty, moody female dressed as a paratrooper.

Luckily, once Suzan had removed the strange headgear, we got chatting and things started to improve. It was an entertaining couple of hours where we clearly started to get on like a house on fire, although Suzan did do most of the talking. She does go into overdrive. (That's no surprise if you've ever met her!) She began by firing certain questions at me. Was I married? Divorced? Did I have kids? She clearly wanted to make sure of my personal situation.

What she didn't do was ask all the usual Slade-related questions or try to dig for anecdotes about people I knew or any kind of celeb gossip. Instead, we discovered a mutual love of Americana music. Even though I already knew of her love of music, the depth of her knowledge of blues, country and old R & B surprised me as she was so much younger. Her dad's music collection and his heroes like Eddie Cochran, Buddy Holly and British artists like Lonnie Donegan had fired that enthusiasm. It showed me that our age difference was no barrier to discussion. She was twenty-four when we met and had been a news journalist before moving into TV production. This background meant she had a broad understanding of many things going on in the world, even though we didn't agree on a lot of subjects. We've had many heated debates over the years. I found it very refreshing.

At the end of the evening the awkwardness returned. It was dark by now so I offered to walk Suzan to her car. Clearly the wrong thing to do.

'I walk myself to my car every night, thank you,' she said witheringly. 'I can manage perfectly well by myself!'

Okaaaay. I went to say goodbye, what should I do now? A little kiss? Shake her hand?...Salute? After all, she was back in paratrooper mode.

I decided on the little kiss, bent forward, puckered the lips, was firmly offered one chaste cheek for half a second, and she was gone into the darkness.

Now, I wasn't to know but Suzan had thoroughly enjoyed our evening. She hid it well. She was quite taken by me, she has revealed since, and was absolutely certain that we had made a connection and that I would ring her on the following day to set up another date.

Trouble was, I didn't ring her. Not the next day nor the day after that. I was intending to, once I could get round to it, but I was busy working. There was no way for Suzan to know that, of course. As the days hurtled towards the weekend and she realized that she still had not given me her home number, she started to panic. Looking back over the date – how it had started, the way she had behaved and what she'd been wearing – made her more and more convinced that the chances of me calling her were distinctly unlikely.

She told me later, 'I got myself into a total state. What on earth had I been thinking? I'd played it so cool I was practically frostbitten. Why on earth would anyone come back for more? I was so desperate for you to call me that I drove everyone mad, I couldn't eat, I couldn't sleep, I couldn't work.' By the Friday lunchtime her workmates had had enough and told her to bite the bullet and just call me herself. I answered and this very hesitant voice launched into 'Hi, Noddy, this is Suzan . . . Suzan Price . . . I work at *Central Weekend Live* . . . we met up this week for a drink.'

It was hard to stop myself from laughing. 'Yes, Suzan, hi, I know who you are. I do remember you.' *How could I forget?* 'I'm not quite at the senile stage yet.'

'Oh right, good. Well, I was just wondering, I mean it's fine if you don't want to, I mean, I completely understand if you don't, but I was thinking, there's this movie on in Birmingham next week that I think you'll like, if you fancy it, say no if you want, but I just thought, perhaps, if you've nothing better to do you might, well, what I'm trying to say is . . .' I did say she goes into overdrive.

I decided to put her out of her misery. 'Yes, that sounds good. I was going to call you, actually. A film next week would be great.'

We arranged to meet up at the cinema over the road from the studios. Suzan decided to approach the second date a little differently. She arrived that night in make-up, a short black dress, stockings and high heels. She looked hot. As she walked towards me I whispered to myself… 'Got her!'

Within a couple of years of us being together, Suzan, in her more usual forthright manner, broached the subject of us having kids.

She'd taken brilliantly to the role of step-mum to Charisse and Jess, who were in their early teens when we met, and had established an excellent relationship with my ex-wife Leandra too. Of all the people we knew, Leandra seemed to understand our relationship from the very beginning. She seemed to 'get' why we were together and wasn't blinded by the difference in our ages. For some men having their ex and current wives strike up a friendship can be intimidating. I like to think it shows my excellent taste in women. (That's the right answer, isn't it, ladies?)

Anyway, Suzan sat me down and asked me straight if I could ever see us having a baby. It might sound daft but even though I knew she was in her twenties and clearly had a strong maternal side, I'd never given the matter any serious thought up to that point. Most men don't really think like that. We are more impulsive creatures and don't dwell on the 'ifs and maybes' of the future.

I told her I'd have to think about it, this was a big decision, and in what must have been an almost supernatural show of restraint, for her, she did not bring up the subject again for a long time. She carried on concentrating on her career.

Suzan swore that whatever I decided she would understand and she wasn't about to up and leave if I said I didn't want a baby. I believed she meant what she said. Age and experience also told me that if I said no to trying for a baby, our relationship would be put under great strain. If I wasn't prepared to consider having another child as I approached fifty then I really should have thought better of dating a girl in her twenties! I knew that denying Suzan the chance to be a mother would break her heart.

I gave the matter a lot of serious thought over a long time. It wasn't only becoming a father again that I had to think about. Age didn't seem too much of a problem, yet. Would that be the same when I was sixty and she was forty? It was too difficult to imagine all the possible scenarios. There are so many variables in any relationship. We were not the first to be in this situation and certainly won't be the last. The bottom line is: do you love one another? That's all that really counts. I think Joan Collins has the right attitude to age-difference relationships. When news broke that she was to marry her fifth husband, Percy Gibson, a man thirty-two years her junior, a reporter asked her if she was worried about the age difference.

'If he dies, he dies,' said Joan.

Once I'd made my mind up that we would try for a baby, as with my attitude to everything else, I didn't hang about.

Suzan had a straightforward pregnancy and her due date was in early January. That brought back memories of the births of my daughters. Charisse was due on Christmas Day 1976, and Leandra and I spent a very nervous Christmas with me not having any booze at all in case she went into labour and I needed to rush her to hospital. In the end Charisse arrived the day after Boxing Day, a little late, but still the best Christmas present. When Jessica came along twenty months later, I was even allowed to help in the delivery. Magical! I, of course, went around telling everybody, 'I could have been a surgeon if I'd wanted to, you know. Dr Holder has a certain ring to it.'

The first Suzan and I knew that our baby was on the way was a Saturday evening just after watching *Blind Date* on TV. She came into the kitchen and announced, 'I think my waters have broken.'

I was a bit confused. 'You think? Well, have they or haven't they?'

Suzan got defensive. 'I don't know. It's all right for you, I've never done this before!'

As she moved around the bedroom gathering up the stuff she needed for hospital Suzan started to yell for help. The more she moved, the more her waters broke. I was in a state of panic too. We'd not long had a new bedroom carpet!

On the way to hospital Suzan was obviously tense so I tried to lighten the mood. Unfortunately every time I made her laugh she lost a bit more fluid. Soggy leggings on a frosty January night are apparently not a very pleasant experience, so she kept alternating from laughing to getting very cross.

The staff at the hospital were great and quickly made Suzan comfortable for the night. She was contracting and in labour but was able to sleep for a while so I was told to go home and get some rest while I could. By the time I got back at breakfast time the following day, Suzan's contractions were coming thick and fast and she had been moved into the delivery suite. We had been told the baby would be due by that evening, but clearly no one had told the baby. This child wasn't planning to hang about. Having a baby is the best experience (well, I hardly felt a thing) and as this was my third time I felt I knew the drill. Being supportive and encouraging is the dad's role, so I was as supportive and encouraging as I knew how to be: 'COME ONNNN . . . THAT'S IT . . . NOW PUUUSSHHH! . . . PUSH HARDER!'

Suzan never said a word but one look said it all. She was completely mortified that everyone in the hospital and probably everyone in the whole of the surrounding area knew that she was attempting to give birth to Noddy Holder's child. My distinctive vocal style was not working in my favour on this occasion. Windows were shattering and small animals were running for cover.

It worked, though, and the baby arrived with a whoosh. We hadn't known whether we were having a boy or a girl and it was such a thrill when the nurse said, 'It's a boy.' As he was handed to me it was hard to take in. He looked just like a mini me, a Holder through and through.

We'd known all along that if it was a boy we would call him Django, in homage to the gypsy jazz guitarist Django Reinhardt. I'd always loved the name. Reinhardt was a Paris-based musician, famous in the 1930s and 1940s, and played with violinist Stéphane Grappelli in the Quintette du Hot Club de France. I have loved their music from a teenager when my mentor on the guitar, the sadly departed Freddie Degville, himself a great jazz player, turned me on to this gypsy swing. It's incredible that Reinhardt, with such talent, had a disfigured left hand. He was injured, aged eighteen, in a fire in his caravan and no one thought he'd ever play music again. He relearned to play with just two fingers and became Europe's top jazz musician.

Django was a good baby with all ten fingers and ten toes in place. He was a character from day one with the ability to make you laugh and always had a thing about dressing up in costume, as kids do. You never knew what he was going to appear as next. A cowboy, Spider-Man, Zorro, Harry Potter . . . I lost track of how many mornings I was woken by a knight in armour poking his plastic sword into my leg beneath the duvet because he wanted Dad to join him in his latest quest for adventure.

He began to learn to play guitar when he was at primary school but I never pushed him into it. I don't think music should become a chore. Even when he started having proper guitar lessons I wouldn't let him study for exams or grades right away. I just wanted him to play for fun and discover what he liked for himself. I'd find him rifling through my CD collection when he started to get really serious about playing. He was about twelve and never went a day without picking up a guitar. He started researching bands and styles of music he had heard me talk about. He went through the Beatles' back catalogue and loved Oasis, then got into the heavy rock stuff like AC/DC and Guns N' Roses; next it was Johnny Cash – a real eclectic mix. He taught himself some piano and is a mean thumper on drums.

When he was born I swore I would never take a job that would take me away from the family for more than a fortnight at a time and I've been able to stick to that. The girls took to having a baby brother wonderfully. I think Charisse was initially a bit worried about whether it would affect my relationship with them. She was nineteen when he came along but she was still the big sister looking out for her and Jess. She may also have been mildly horrified at the evidence that her dad was still having sex, of course.

The fact is that my being around more for Django meant I was around more for them too. These days they might not need their dad in quite the same way, but they know I'm always there for them. It comes full circle in the end: Charisse now needs regular help with babysitting since the arrival of my first grandchild, the completely irresistible Isabelle.

I realize I'm very lucky to have a blended family that works. Almost everyone I know who has a first, second and even third family has had nightmare scenarios. If you leave your wife or husband for someone else that is obviously likely to cause trouble and luckily that's not what happened to us.

I don't have any amazing secret to reveal on how we made it work, but don't bad-mouth each other to your kids. They don't need to be caught up in the details of the split. You may not be able to live together any more, but you both still love the kids and need to keep a healthy respect for the mother or father of your children.

Young people tend to delay getting married these days until they are a little older. Consequently there has been a drop of 25 per cent in divorces within the first seven years, that dreaded seven-year itch, and a 50 per cent drop within the first three years. That said, a child born today only has a fifty-fifty chance of their parents still being together by the time they are sixteen years old.

The world may be rapidly changing but what people go through with their families and children has stayed very much the same for everyone.

When Charisse was little she was asked to write a diary piece one Monday morning at school and describe what she had done over the weekend. When Leandra went to pick her up that day she was horrified to find that Charisse had written a detailed account of a party we had thrown, ending with 'everyone was very noisy and kept me and my sister awake all night and my Daddy was so drunk he fell down the stairs and landed on his head. He says this is what has sent him silly.' The raised eyebrow of the schoolteacher had Leandra worrying that a call to social services could well be on the cards.

More than twenty years later Django was asked to write a diary entry on exactly the same subject. (How nosy are these teachers? Maybe they think there is some sort of rock 'n' roll orgy going on every weekend at Holder Towers.) He gave a thrilling description of a Guy Fawkes party at my mates Helen and Pete Mitchell's house. Now, radio presenter Pete is a bit of a pyromaniac on the quiet and lives up to my nickname for him on bonfire nights:

Pyro Pete. He loves huge fireworks and is a bit gung-ho about how he sets up the annual display in his garden. We have to keep the kids well back.

On this particular night Pete excelled himself. The fireworks had all gone off without a hitch (or even, one could say, with a bang!). The discarded remains of the spent cases of Catherine wheels, bangers, rockets and fountains were littering the garden and all of a sudden, in a brain-dead moment, Pissed Up Pyro Pete became a Womble. He gathered up all the firework debris...only to throw it into a still-blazing chimenea. So basically, he threw a load of gunpowder remnants on to a fire. As we realized what he was doing we all shouted 'Nooooo ...!' but too late. The stone patio heater started to crackle and explode. Suddenly one particular rocket erupted into new life and shot out of the side of the fire's flaming mouth, straight towards me, as if I was a projectile magnet. The rest of the party had already headed for the hills.

As Django later explained to his rather unimpressed schoolteacher: 'My daddy tried to run away but he fell over on the slippery grass and we all laughed when a rocket shot right up his bottom!' Oh yes, how we all laughed. Out of the mouths of babes...

Chapter Four

I'M STILL STANDING
YEAH YEAH YEAH

All the world's a stage, And all the men and women merely players.

As You Like It by William Shakespeare

I'm not often given to quoting from Shakespeare. I rarely drop out a 'verily' or a 'forsooth' but for the subject I'm about to talk about it seems to sum things up nicely.

No one knows what life can hold in store when they begin to make their way in the world. I believe your environment does have a lasting effect on the person you become, along with the experiences you have. The most important factor that truly defines the life you will live, however, is the choices you make.

The choice I made that totally defined my life was when I decided to leave school at sixteen to become a professional musician. It was 1962. In those days to be a musician wasn't as simple as it might sound today. You may as well have announced you were going to become a vagrant and a bum. In most people's opinion it amounted to the same thing. There was no security to be found in being a singer. It seemed a precarious and dangerous thing to want to be and no way to earn a living.

I'd been a pretty good student – I'd got six O-levels (as GCSEs were called in those days) and began to study A-levels in sixth form. My overall obsession, though, was music. The career advisors' only advice for a working-class lad with O-levels was to work in a bank or become a teacher. I enjoyed history lessons at school and flirted with the idea of teaching history. I think I would have made a good teacher, but in those teenage years it was only music that filled my mind, body and soul. It made me feel complete. Hearing Little Richard sing 'The Girl Can't Help It' in 1957 rocked my world. Things would never be the same again.

My parents were shocked when I said I wanted to leave school. I was gigging regularly around the Midlands with my band, the Rockin' Phantoms (how's that for a cool name?), and consequently falling well behind with my A-level work. My mum was a school cleaner, my dad a window cleaner and pop music wasn't something they would ever consider to be a wise career move. Full credit to them, though – after prolonged, heated discussions they didn't try to stop me. It was a world completely alien to them and I doubt they thought I would succeed anyway. They just thought I needed a couple of years to get it out of my system before settling down to a 'proper job'.

Whatever their motivation, it was a wise choice, eventually. It's very hard to stand back and let young people have their own way. Parents do think they know best and it's all too easy to lay down the law and try to force kids to make the choices you want them to make. That doesn't allow for their own personality or who they might turn out to be in future.

There was always a voice inside telling me music was the key to my destiny. My mum was worried, I know, but much of my dad's youth had been spent fighting overseas for six years during the Second World War, with many of his pals being killed and their bodies not coming home. After a cruel experience like that his attitude was 'Go for it, you can always do something else if it doesn't work out. That way you can't say you didn't give it a shot.' I'll always be grateful to my folks. If they'd been the sort of parents who had said a definite 'No' to me leaving school, and if they had not supported me along the way, it would have made our relationship very difficult.

I've always tried hard to do the same with my three kids. They have made their own career choices and I will give them advice only when they ask. They all have a strong work ethic and have been successful in their own right. People think I have opened doors for them but nothing could be further from the truth. Everything they have achieved has come entirely through their own efforts.

I know people who struggle to understand the choices their kids make. It is one of the hardest things about being a parent – to let them try and sort out what they want to do. I'm not sure teachers help too much with the process either. They certainly didn't when I was at school. If you weren't so studious they simply opened the school gates, said 'Bye bye', and expected you to walk straight into some sort of factory apprenticeship. In the Midlands there were lots of opportunities in those days in engineering, car manufacture and foundries. My home town of Walsall specialized in the leather industry, hence the football team's nickname 'The Saddlers'.

The world is very different now. No job is 'secure' in the same way and people don't have jobs for life the way they used to. The careers advice offered by schools doesn't seem to have moved forward much, though. The bright kids are now all funnelled towards universities, whether or not they want or need a degree. Apprenticeships and training for skilled work are hard to find and there's little guidance available for those who may be more suited to that kind of work.

There can still be a lot of resistance to my field, which today is called the 'performing arts', as a serious career.

I meet lots of kids who are talented singers, dancers, musicians and actors, and many tell me that they struggle to find any decent advice at school about how to pursue a career in the arts. There are more subjects now available to study, so many more than I ever had. Music lessons when I was at school were just choir practice, and if you were lucky you got to bang the one and only tambourine. Now there's music technology, media studies in TV and radio, and theatre studies that can cover much more than just acting, but also design, sound, lighting and direct-ing. The trouble with a lot of these courses, if you ask me (and as the book is called *The World According to Noddy* clearly someone *has* asked me), is that sometimes they are taught by teachers who have no real understanding of the reality of working in the arts in the big wide world, and the spin-offs that are available.

Parents can be surprisingly prejudiced against kids wanting to pursue their future in these areas. They still believe, just as my parents did, that most people don't have a cat in hell's chance of making it in show business. I think it depends what you mean by 'making it'. It's true that only a handful of hopefuls are ever going to become Oscar-winning actors or Grammy award-winning musi-cians. It's scary when I hear from my actor friends that 92 per cent of the profession are out of work at any one time and even scarier, when that figure is broken down, that the remaining 8 per cent tend to get the most work and the others don't get much of a look in. You obviously have to strive to join that 8 per cent.

Even performers at the top of the tree have had to start somewhere, though. The real question is whether all these youngsters have the passion for theatre, dance or music that means they are going to find a way to make a career in that world, whatever it takes. This is where parents and teachers often make a mistake. There are lots of opportunities to change course if things are not going as planned. Working behind the scenes in production, stage management, sound, lighting, design, make-up and wardrobe are an essential part of a theatre, film or TV crew. You don't hear so much about those career paths but they all exist and there are plenty more. I have friends who started out in bands and weren't able to make a living wage as musicians, but went on to become managers, agents, publicists and touring technicians. In one case a musician friend, who was absolutely broke, started a tour catering company with a little van and a few quid I loaned her to buy saucepans, knives and suchlike. She now has a thriving little empire employing many people.

So anything can be achieved through hard work: the avenues are there and wide open.

If you've got a kid who is talented in the arts, but I have to stress also 100 per cent committed and not just sitting on their derrière, they can find a way forward. What's the point of insisting they study chemistry, sociology or Mandarin Chinese if they are no good at it, just so they have options? Maybe the only thing that is going to satisfy them is being involved with *putting on a show*, in whatever form that takes. I say give them the best chance possible by letting them study the subjects at which they are good. This is where they will excel. Support them when they want to join the drama club or have music lessons or go to dance class. Take them to the theatre, even if it's just the local amateur dramatics production.

I get told all the time that success in show business is all down to luck. I absolutely do not agree. You have to be prepared to put everything you have into it, go the extra mile, make yourself stand out. Show everyone why you are the best. Learn as much as you can, get as many experiences doing whatever it is you love. Go and sweep the stage or sell programmes at your local theatre at weekends. Watch bands play in the pub down the road. Learn the tricks of the trade. Whether it's dancing, acting, singing or getting hold of a camera and making little films, do it, do it again and then do it some more. Build up a portfolio, get references from people you work alongside, ask questions and listen to the answers.

A lucky break is all very nice. Yes, we do all need one at some point in our lives, but a lucky break isn't going to be enough in itself. Most of all you have to be able to take advantage of the opportunity, capitalize on it and live up to it if you want to be there for the long haul.

I know very many talented musicians who have never achieved huge fame and fortune. Now, some might not have that elusive commodity that is 'star quality', whatever that may be. Simon Cowell is still trying to track it down every year on TV's *The X Factor*. Lack of success can more than likely rest on the inability to translate a 'lucky break' into the big time.

That said, ask most musicians, actors or dancers and they'll tell you that if they can make a living within the business some way, it still beats any other job they would want. In the end, it is about what makes you happy. I'll say it again, y'all.

I could have been fulfilled being a history teacher, I know I would have enjoyed it, but then you wouldn't have had this book to read. You, boy! Yes, you at the back...did you hear what I said?

Going back to Shakespeare (perhaps I have indeed missed my calling to be a schoolmaster), he described life as having seven distinct stages in 'The Seven Ages of Man', a monologue in *As You Like It*. Those ages roughly translate into: Infancy, Schoolboy, Lover, Soldier, Wiseman and Old Age before returning at the end of life to Infancy and dependency again.

Recently I came across a more modern interpretation of the ageing process written by journalist Virginia

Ironside. Her version read: Lager, Aga, Saga, Viagra, Gaga. I'll leave you to speculate on where you think I am in that process at the moment.

I wonder if the pop-star lifecycle of the modern era could be boiled down into an even more succinct three ages: Wannabe, It's All About Me and, very quickly in most cases, Who Was He/She?

Whichever way you choose to look at it there is one inevitable conclusion to be drawn. Ageing is a fact of life for everyone. In the words of Benjamin Franklin: 'Nothing can be said to be certain, except death and taxes.'

Getting older isn't something that I've ever worried too much about. I can't see the point in fretting about something I can't prevent. As it's often said, growing older is better than the alternative, anyway.

Having a wife who is twenty years younger might make me think about the ageing process a bit more, perhaps, but why should I worry? I have a wife who is twenty years younger than me!

I should be so lucky, lucky, lucky, lucky.

It does make me cross when I see a certain kind of reporting on the ageing of people in the public eye.

Suzan and I always put the TV news on first thing in the morning and channel hop between the news channels. One morning we saw a showbiz report from New

York of a reunion of the original cast of the 1972 film *Cabaret*. Now, *Cabaret* is my favourite film; I must have seen it a hundred times. There was a time I could recite the whole script and knew every song and scene off by heart. I even hosted the fortieth anniversary TV tribute on BBC2's *The Culture Show*. The morning news report showed a photo of its star Liza Minnelli alongside the actor who played her love interest, Michael York, and Joel Grey, who was the emcee in the movie.

We were horrified to see the presenter and guest newspaper reviewers on the show snorting with laughter at the sight of the mature stars, in particular, Michael York.

'Ooh, what a shame, he doesn't look as handsome as he used to,' one snobby, self-appointed know-it-all said.

'Oh dear, how awful, doesn't he look old?' said another.

Even the presenter, a man with suspiciously dark hair probably not as old as he is, joined in. He zoomed in on his iPad so we could all get a good look at the actor on our TV screens. An actor, can I remind everyone, who was being compared to how he looked in a film made over *forty* years earlier. Now, I don't know what planet these cackling idiots live on, but I don't know *anyone* who looks the same as they did forty years ago, whoever they are. There was absolutely nothing wrong with the way Michael York looked. He was smart, distinguished and still handsome. His only crime was to look older. Unforgiveable! Now, this item was being explored on a 'news' programme. I don't know about you, but I don't think the fact that people age over a forty-year period is news. If he hadn't aged a day over those forty years, now *that* would be news! My wife Suzan, an ex-journalist herself, was so incensed at the treatment of Michael York, she immediately emailed her views to the newsroom. Of course, they weren't read out. So much for a balanced viewpoint.

I was probably boring Liza Minnelli senseless about how much I luuurved *Cabaret* when I eventually met her at some boozy event. She said self-mockingly of herself by referring to the characters in *The Wizard of Oz*, starring her mother Judy Garland: 'I'm Dorothy's daughter up top, but the Tin Man down below!' This is after being a dancer all her life – as a result of entertaining us, she has crushed discs, metal plates screwed into her body, two false hips and a wired-up knee. She has problems going through the scanner at airports, I bet.

These snide reviewers haven't got a clue. You see it all the time in newspapers, too – some film star pictured many years after their youthful heyday with a 'Look what's happened to so and so ...' headline.

I'm probably lucky not to have been the victim of that sort of ridiculous attack too often. Or maybe I have and I just haven't come across it. There are not enough hours in the day to be trawling for nasty gossip on social media about myself, written by cowards who know nothing about me. Don't feel the need to email me a link to anything I may have missed... no, really, don't!

Cut me and I'll bleed. Try to hurt me with words and it'll be empty vessels making the most noize.

Luckily I'm tough enough to take it anyway. I'm going through my sixties at the same time as a lot of my mates. I'm surprised to find that not many of them are planning to carry on celebrating birthdays, even the ones only going into their fifties. I'm still up for getting family and friends together for a noisy bash, lots to eat and drink, dancing and playing music into the early hours, a proper party. Quite frankly, I'm thankful I'm still standing at sixty-eight to have a party, considering the life I've led.

Not that there aren't things about ageing that do bother me. There's nothing fun about anything that compromises your health. I have to make far more trips to the opticians and the dentist than I used to. My doctor is always nagging me to watch how much sugar I eat and keep an eye on my blood pressure.

I was chatting with American rock drummer Carmine Appice not so long ago. Carmine has been on the road since the sixties and worked with Black Sabbath and Jeff Beck amongst others, and co-wrote 'Da Ya Think I'm Sexy?' with Rod Stewart. He said to me: 'In the old days on the road the talk used to be all about what drugs everyone was doing, which were the ones that got you most high. Now all we do is compare our blood pressure tablets and cholesterol medication.'

There are other things that let you know you're getting older too...but I can't remember what they are...Oh, yes...memory! Your memory plays tricks on you all the time. Luckily it only seems to affect the more trivial parts of my life. Trying to recall the name of an actor in a film you watched the night before, that sort of thing. The more important stuff from way back seems to be much more fixed in place. I guess your head gets filled with more and more facts, memories and rubbish, and as you get older it decides to jettison some of the more superfluous stuff to make room for the things you really need to remember. Anyway, that's my story and I'm sticking to it.

When my mum was an old lady she was a classic Mrs Malaprop, getting all her words mixed up. There were times when you knew what she was trying to say and she'd get pretty close but never get it quite right. She always insisted on calling Suzi Quatro 'Suzi Cointreau' and Alvin Stardust was 'Albert Starbrush'. I've never told Alvin but I'm sure he's been called worse in his time. She would go all of a quiver when the pop group Wet Wet Wet came on TV, especially lead singer Marti Pellow...'that nice Martian Pillow, he's lovely and you can hear all the words when he sings, you know'. She'd love Michael Bublé if she was still around now. He'd be right up her street and he would of course be 'Mikey Bubbly' or 'Bubblegum'.

For some reason Mum's pronunciation of broccoli was always broc-i-o-lie and chicken biryani was origami. Ever since she died, all the family still use the mispronunciations and we all smile to one another. Ma Holder's theory whenever she saw anything about climate change was 'I blame them Sputniks the Russians sent up into space in the sixties, messing about with nature. It's not normal.' She may have a point. Another classic that had everyone doubled up with laughter was when we were talking about plans for the New Year in 2000. She'd heard all the news reports about everything going haywire at the dawn of the new millennium, computers crashing, planes falling from the sky, all that sort of rubbish. She got herself all worked up, 'I just don't know what's going to happen to the world when that new linoleum comes in!'

According to the family I am starting to fall into this habit myself. The trouble is, when you are the one doing the talking you have no idea you are doing it. It all makes perfect sense to me. It's only when I see the sniggering and smirking that I realize I've made some sort of verbal cock-up.

Over dinner one night with friends we were talking about the famous Muhammad Ali v. George Foreman fight in Zaire in 1974. 'Ah yes,' I ventured knowledgeably, 'the Mumble in the Jumble.' Now, I know this legendary boxing match has always been known as the 'Rumble in the Jungle' but this is what age, and a couple of very large glasses of wine, can do to a man. I made it sound like a couple of old grannies squabbling over a second-hand cardigan at a car-boot sale.

My own vegetable malapropism is butternut squash. Every now and again it just comes out as 'butternush squat'. What with that and the broc-i-o-lie it can make a visit to the greengrocer's a bit awkward.

Sometimes your hearing can let you down too. I was cooking dinner one night and, in my defence, I was busy. There were pans on the gas hob bubbling away and the extractor fan was on full power, all of which made following what Suzan was trying to tell me a bit tricky. She'd been watching the news headlines and had just heard reports that Colonel Gaddafi had been shot and killed in Libya. She came into the kitchen and said: 'Gaddafi's been shot.' She does just come straight out with things sometimes and expects me to immediately know exactly what's in her brain with no run-up or explanation whatsoever.

'What?' I asked.

'Gaddafi's been shot!' she repeated.

She then looked puzzled as I stared at her in complete horror and said: 'Oh no, that's terrible, what a shame.'

It was Suzan's turn to look confused. 'Well, he was an evil dictator and a mass murderer, I don't know if I'd say it was ... a shame ...'

'Sorry,' I said. 'Who did you say had been shot?'

'Gaddafi,' she said yet again. 'Colonel Gaddafi.' She paused and then asked, 'Who did you *think* I was talking about?'

'Oh, Gaddafi,' I said, hugely relieved. 'I thought you said Dappy, you know, from N-Dubz. I love Dappy, he makes me laugh!'

For some reason Suzan found this exchange completely hilarious.

One of the ageing processes of which I am increasingly aware is how much longer it takes me to get over a drunken night. I remember having some time off during a US tour and flying down to New Orleans to celebrate my thirtieth birthday. I hardly went to bed for five days straight.

*Those were the days my friend, I thought they'd
never end.*

Now a hangover can last days. Maybe in the past I just topped up regularly so it never became a hangover. Now I don't even like to eat a hot curry too late in the evening in case I'm plagued all night with heartburn. Stop sniggering: it will come to you all in good time.

I think I first realized that I was being made to feel old before my time due to my radio work. I worked weekends on commercial radio for sixteen years with my own seventies music and dance party shows. They were networked on stations around the UK and in some areas I regularly beat BBC Radio 1 figures for how many listeners tuned in on Saturday and Sunday nights. Eventually, the powers that be decided not to renew my contract as I didn't match the demographic of the listeners they wanted to attract. The fact that I was popular with all age groups and getting people to tune in didn't seem to matter.

You see it happen all the time in broadcasting. Older, more experienced presenters are moved out to make way for younger people because the bosses think that is what the public wants. You have to bring in new talent, of course – I'm not saying all young presenters on TV and radio are no good – but sometimes the experience and warmth of an older presenter can be overlooked and not valued enough, and you need a balance.

I read an interview with Graham Norton a while ago where he said: 'On the radio show I chatted to Sheila Hancock and Nicholas Parsons. Sheila's 80, Nicholas is 90, both still going strong, and you suddenly realise Wow! There's more time left than you thought.'

Graham is a mere fifty years old. So well said, Graham, you young whippersnapper, you!

Ant and Dec are a great example of younger presenters who are masters of their craft. Mind you, they started out so young they have been doing it for about twenty-five years already. What they have that so many young presenters lack is a warmth and ease to their style of presenting. You feel like you know them – it's a real skill. I worked as their voiceover man on a couple of series of *Saturday Night Takeaway*.

I'm a big fan of presenters Sam and Mark too. Sam Nixon and Mark Rhodes (who's from my hometown of Walsall) got together after competing on *Pop Idol*, back in 2003. They could follow in the footsteps of Ant and Dec, with their natural ability to do comedy alongside their presenting. They do great stuff on kids TV, as do another double act, Dick and Dom. Both pairs have the knack of not talking down to kids, which translates to entertaining adults as well. It would be good to see how they'd fare on primetime TV.

It's not just on screen where everyone seems to be getting younger. Producers in TV and radio are often also very young. This means you can end up with inexperienced people making programmes for a wider audience that is made up of all ages, an audience to which they can't always relate. The ideas they come up with to entertain us, though, are not all cutting edge and new. There are very few brand new ideas. Much of it has been done before in one guise or another. There's nothing wrong with recycling; I'm all for it if it can be made to work.

One of the biggest recycled hits on television is *Strictly Come Dancing*. *Come Dancing* was a show my mum and dad watched since we got a TV set, way back in 1953. Who would have believed that a ballroom show could be reinvented and end up so popular in this day and age? I didn't, for sure. Its success is due largely to the fact that it's a family show every generation can sit and watch together on a Saturday evening. It has high production values and the producers haven't gone down the route of just plucking the latest 'hot' young presenters and grafting them on to the show.

Strictly's Bruce Forsyth is clearly one example of an older broadcaster who bucked the trend and helped the extravaganza prove a ratings winner. He had critics endlessly calling for him to be replaced with claims that he was too old, but he finally decided to call it a day himself at the age of eighty-six. Say what you like about Brucie, he's done primetime TV live on air for decades, and for all the fluffed lines and terrible jokes, he's still miles better than many who sought to replace him. There are presenters a third of his age who make endless cock-ups and can't read their autocue, and they don't get anywhere near the knocks he received. You don't see these fluffs as most shows are pre-recorded and heavily edited. Let's see how they fare doing live TV when they're in their eighties. I doubt their careers on TV will last that long.

Len Goodman, one of the judges on the show, didn't even start his TV panel career until he was into his sixties. He'd worked as a dance professional, teacher and judge until some enterprising producer decided to put him on the programme as the voice of ballroom experience. What a brilliant move and a chance for Len to show there was life in the old dog yet. He himself admits that all the fame and attention he gained might have turned his head if it had happened to him as a young man. The fact that he was older and wiser means he is thoroughly appreciative of the chances he is now being given. He's a judge on the US version of the show as well and commutes across the Atlantic every week to do both versions. It shows the viewers want to be in knowledgeable hands, while Len is also an inspiration to the older generation that it's never too late to try something new.

Flying the flag for the more mature ladies on TV is Mary Berry, another expert in her field and a vital ingredient in the audience-pleasing *Great British Bake Off*. Young or old, cooking fans love her. Respect, Mary.

David Attenborough still has to be surpassed as the presenter of natural history programmes. All these names I have mentioned have one thing in common...they know what they are talking about and can connect that to the audience.

So often you see new talent with ability in one field being pushed into doing far too much, too soon. These days faces become flavour of the month overnight. Suddenly they are on every panel game, talk show or reality programme. It's a case of overkill and performers need to tread very carefully. If they are really unlucky they will suddenly be given their own chat show to host. A poisoned chalice if ever there was one, as many celebrities have found to their cost. Interviewing and making it look effortless is not as easy as it looks.

I always loved working in radio. I was able to indulge my love of music as if I was at home. For my own show I was lucky and allowed to play all the stuff I would want to listen to myself. This included all genres of popular music and my audience seemed to enjoy my choices on two very different shows every weekend.

I do miss the banter with the radio audience and nowadays I certainly wouldn't be given the freedom I had back then to personally choose what I wanted to play. That would kill the attraction for me. Everything now is computerized and constricted and, although I do understand that independent radio stations are at the mercy of advertising revenue and audience research, when you drive up the motorway the different stations you encounter become totally interchangeable. In America in any one city you can pick up pop, country and western, classical, oldies (or 'Gold' as it now known), AOR, heavy rock and a selection of soul stations, as well as talk shows. We don't have anything like that amount of choice here, but then we are only the size of one of their lakes.

The real characters you used to find presenting radio shows are slowly disappearing. Some of the strangest people I have ever encountered have been radio presenters. I'm not completely sure why that is, but I think the fact they spend hours on end in a room talking to themselves must have something to do with it. If they're not bonkers when they start out, they end up that way.

GOOOD MOORRRRRNING
BIIIIIIIIIRMINGHAAAAAAM!

It might be irritating to find that the emphasis is on a younger image when it comes to people working in broadcasting, but when it happens in politics it's downright dangerous!

All the political parties in this country appear to be moving closer together in their policies until they are practically merging as one.

It used to be that if you were a Conservative or a Labour voter it meant something and you knew what it stood for. It's not so easy to tell now.

The prime ministers I remember from my youth were always older gentlemen with some modicum of wisdom under their belts. You didn't see them flaunting themselves around with showbiz types. They appeared to be above all that stuff. Men like Winston Churchill,

Clement Attlee and Harold Macmillan. They seemed to believe in their principles. I was actually named after another, Neville Chamberlain. (My name is not Noddy, surprisingly…No, honestly! I'm Neville John on my birth certificate.)

The most important factor when selecting a candidate to run for leader of a political party now seems to be whether or not they are young and televisual. Will they look good in photos? Do they know how to talk in soundbites? You can be very bright and have had a brilliant education, but where does the global knowledge you need to lead a country come from? You only learn from experience. We are talking about how to deal with various governments and cultures all over the world, disasters, wars, economies and all manner of situations. If history teaches us nothing else, it's that history constantly repeats itself. You have to have lived through upheavals a few times before you can steer the population down the right road.

> *The farther backward you can look, the farther forward you are likely to see.*
>
> Winston Churchill

It's argued that parties feel they have to have a candidate who appeals to women and the youth vote. That seems very superficial and an insult to those voters. Why is the opinion of the older generation side-lined? They are the ones more likely to go to the polling booths. It's no wonder there are so many political scandals. Power corrupts in any field, but I don't see this as acceptable. An older person may well be more equipped to deal with that power.

I see prime ministers and politicians from the past thirty years who pop up on current affairs debates, and years after they have left office they talk a lot more sense than they ever did when they were in power.

John Major, Gordon Brown and William Hague all appear much more confident and self-assured as they get older than they ever did when they were actually leading their parties. Maybe when the pressure's off we get the truth and we warm to them more.

I wonder if looking back Tony Blair ever regrets his 'Cool Britannia' episode. When Labour came to power in 1997 he invited a load of pop stars, actors, fashion designers and what the politicians must have considered 'cool' people for a drinks party at Number 10. It made quite a spectacle as MPs and suited civil servants tried to convince us they were 'trendy and with it' by hobnobbing with the showbiz set. What a load of bollocks!

Now if I ruled the world...

Chapter Five

THIS IS THE MODERN WORLD

Let me state for the record, I have not, nor have I ever had, a personal account on Facebook or Twitter.

If you go and look, no doubt you will find lots of me. Using my name and various pictures of me, various accounts proclaim themselves to be 'Noddy Holder', and they may even have my birthday or 'born in Walsall' as part of their profile. But they are *not* me!

I don't know what benefit the people behind these fake identities get by pretending to be me in cyberspace. Are they spouting nonsense that involves Christmas and drinking cup-a-soups while wearing kipper ties? There was one particular case where a fake 'Noddy Holder' duped more than 4,000 people into believing he or she was me and was even being followed by people who knew me, until they worked out the truth.

I understand the benefits of keeping contact with family and friends scattered around the globe on Facebook. And if you are famous you have large numbers of fans wanting to know what you are up to, that I get. It is a human instinct to want to be part of a tribe.

As for myself, I have no interest whatsoever in invading my own privacy to give detailed accounts of what I've just had for breakfast. Bacon and egg sandwich, if you want to know. Oh, you didn't... fair enough, why would you? I'm not the slightest bit interested in what you had for your breakfast either.

How did this trend start for tracking yourself from coffee shop, to cinema, to bar, with a rundown of all the places you visit along the way? Doesn't anyone ever worry that letting everyone know you're not at home could be an invitation for burglars to pop over and help themselves to the new flatscreen TV you told everyone you bought last week? Mark my words, the time will come when it'll be used as some thief's defence in a court case. Some clever lawyer will argue that a person's constant posting of a detailed schedule on when their home is available to burgle means that the poor victim of a break-in should be blamed for the crime themselves. It'll be said that they incited the burglar to commit the crime. The world is going mad, don't forget.

Facebook posts often cover the most mundane of matters. When you meet up with real, living, breathing friends do you show them pictures of cake? Well, do you? We all know that even our best friends probably have no interest at all in our holiday snaps, and certainly no interest at all in what we've had for a snack. So why should the world want to know?

The separation from how people behave in *real* life and how people behave on the internet not only confuses me, it's worrying. It is much easier for people to say dreadful, hurtful things on social media and think they can get away with it. Some believe they can post whatever they like without worrying about the effect and consequences their words will have on the recipient and their family. Whether it is just a nasty tweet about someone's appearance or a comment that is far more sinister or even libellous, the internet can give anonymity to cowardly posters. There are now far more cases of people being held to account or even prosecuted over such things. Nasty gossip when you are down the pub is one thing, but when your written words are being broadcast globally within seconds you have to be careful. I don't think people yet understand the difference between having an opinion and sharing that belief with the world on social media. Tell you what, here's a brand new theory to ponder on...How about if people keep their nasty opinions to themselves in the first place and be nice to one another? That could work!

*The object of existence is to increase the sum of
human happiness.*

The lack of control over social media sites is out of
hand. It seems the creation of websites and rapid developments in technology have caught everyone unawares.
Governments, laws and agencies that are meant to
monitor and protect people have been left way behind
as the internet becomes more and more of an uncivilized
and anarchic world where none of the usual morals
and social codes apply. If we have the technology and
intelligence to invent such things, why do we not also
have the ability to make sure they are run responsibly?

Now and again I find it mildly amusing to Google
myself or check my Wikipedia page and discover bizarre
details that have been completely invented and presented
as facts. If people want to believe I trained with the
Bolshoi Ballet or have the ability to juggle fire, it doesn't
keep me awake at night. (I sleep quite well considering
the pain in my toes from being *en pointe* all day and
don't get me started on how singed my fingers get!)
Unfortunately not all inaccuracies are as innocent or
amusing. This modern juggernaut of 'free speech' needs
some intelligent restraint, and meanwhile lives are being
wrecked.

The 'over-sharing' that social media encourages can
be the most damaging for youngsters who have yet to

find their feet in an always changing world. For them, the constant posts and pictures of 'friends' having what appears to be fun-filled, action-packed lives can create a real sense of dissatisfaction with their own existence. They have yet to learn not to trust the version of the lives they are being shown. Social media, after all, does not give a realistic view, but an edited, curated one that shows the world only the version the poster wishes us to see.

The effect on impressionable young minds can be terrible. Depression is on the increase amongst our teenagers; every week we read reports of another young boy or girl who has taken their own life. According to studies the more users look at these websites, the worse they feel about themselves.

Those statistics are worrying. Life is for living, but capturing the moment on your phone or iPad now seems to be more important to people than living and enjoying it. Have you been to a gig lately? It's impossible to see whoever is on the stage as they are hidden from view by the sea of camera phones and tablets being held in the air, filming footage no one is ever going to watch. I've seen advertised a three-foot telescopic pole that you can now attach to your device and hold aloft so yours is the highest. Part of the audience just seems desperate to get a shot they can post in the next two minutes to tell everyone where they are. The rest of us are forced into watching the concert through the multitude of fuzzy screens waving back and forth in front of our eyes. Madness! (Not Madness the band, although I'm sure Suggs and the lads suffer this fate as much as any other act.)

This mass addiction to screens of all shapes and sizes is obvious wherever you are. It's illegal to use your phone, unless it's hands free, when you are driving. Yet you still see every other car with someone holding their phone to their ear, tapping away, using their elbows to steer while drinking from a can or coffee cup, eating some snack or applying make-up, often all at the same time and sometimes even with kids in the car. It's mental seeing lives put at risk.

When I rule the world I am going to have every car interior built so that no phone signal can penetrate to a handheld device. This will also serve as sound insulation. I won't have to endure other people's choice of music at full blast and with maximum bass boom when I'm outside their vehicle, either as a driver in my own car or as I'm strolling down the street minding my own business. Their sound system will also be put out of action as soon as they take the roof off the car if it's a convertible. Also, there will be an adapter so, as the roaring acceleration noise from a suped-up exhaust system gets louder and louder, it will cut down the power of the engine, gradually reducing the motor's maximum speed to only 20 mph.

'Stop showing off... We're not looking at you... You're just a KNOBHEAD!... with a small knob.'

Roads are dangerous enough but what about the pavement? Even walking down the street you take your life in your hands as people are so fixated on their phone or tablet they don't bother to look where they are going. People of all ages with vacant expressions, eyes glued to a screen, squinting and frowning over the latest update from whomever, thumbs twitching and tapping in the reply that cannot wait. Accident and emergency must be full of messaging mishaps.

I was walking along a high street one afternoon and coming towards me was a cyclist at full speed, riding on the pavement. Since when were pavements meant for cyclists? Anyway, he was steering one-handed and tapping away on his phone with the thumb of his other hand. As he was swaying all over the place he knocked over an elderly lady carrying her shopping. Her bags went everywhere and I don't think he even noticed or cared. He certainly didn't attempt to stop. As the speedo merchant got next to me, with a bit of nifty thrusting, I stuck out my rolled-up umbrella and rammed the metal tip into the spokes of his front wheel. He crashed across the handlebars, with the bike landing on top of him. Ooh, I bet it hurt! I pinched his ear as hard as I could, and dragged him back to the pensioner. He was more shocked than anything. To a gathering crowd's applause,

I made him pick up all the lady's groceries. The damage to his bicycle and how his bruises must have felt next day taught him a lesson, I hope. They don't call me the ace swordsman for nothing.

What on earth can be so urgent that folk can't wait a few minutes to make a call or read an email? Are these people the head of the United Nations? Or trying to broker a deal for world peace? They can't all be doing something that important that it can't wait a few minutes. Did life, before the mobile age, suddenly come to a standstill if we didn't answer immediately?

The Quiet Zone coach on a train also reveals some people at their worst. They think 'silent' restrictions can't possibly apply to them. I don't want to hear some plonker telling his boss how he's been a whizz-kid at meetings that day and done the deal of the century. It's definitely of no interest to me to hear a loudmouth discussing with the wife what wine they'll be having with dinner when he gets home. Nor do I want to listen to the latest Coldplay spillage from some tinny headphones. Give us some peace, please, we've all had a busy day; it's called the Quiet Zone for a reason. Screechy man, yes, you there, please go and use your phone in a carriage where it's allowed and where other passengers are boring the pants off one another with their devices as well. There you can all battle to be the loudest to your heart's content.

I know I co-wrote a song called 'Cum on Feel the Noize' forty-odd years ago but I never expected it to become a reality outside of a rock venue!

If you are wondering how I know so much about Facebook and Twitter, when I don't partake in their delights myself, the answer is simple. My family are all addicted to social media and talk about it endlessly, whether I want to know about it or not. This is the modern world but as yet I have not succumbed to it.

You can't even watch TV without being greeted by a presenter with their head down, reading out tweets and emails from their laptop or tablet. Is anything 'Shirley from Sheffield' has to say about David Beckham's new tight underpants the key piece of information I'm waiting for? No.

When I was King of Sizzle during Sausage Week... Whoah there!... I bet you had to go back and read that statement again. That's right... I was King of Sizzle during Sausage Week! How could you have missed it? Shame on you! You must have realized by now I do sometimes lead a strange life.

Sausage Week happens every autumn and a couple of years back I was the figurehead of the campaign, with the enviable task of touring the UK to taste sausages made by local butchers to find the best British banger and to encourage the public to buy British food produce.

In one week I must have tasted at least a hundred different varieties of sausage from ye olde traditional to every combination of herbs and spices imaginable. What's not to like? We went all over the country in the Sausage Mobile, a specially designed coach carrying me and all the promotion staff. We had all the latest technology on board and via screens all around us we could monitor every mention of Sausage Week on any form of media. I have to say it was mindboggling to a techno Philistine, namely me. There were TV and radio interviews and photo calls in every city. The media dubbed me 'King of Sizzle' at one point as I posed with platefuls of steaming sausages, a moniker that I think rather suits me.

Looking for some hot stuff baby this evening!

During one long day of sausage eating, and meeting and greeting farmers and butchers, I climbed back on board the bus ready to head off to our next destination.

'Oh, Noddy, you're trendy, you're trendy!' exclaimed the group of young women working on the tour. They were all flustered and excited, and I must admit I was a sight to behold in my mustard-yellow check suit and hat at a jaunty angle. I thought to myself, 'Ah, the boy can't help it, I've still got IT!' Not only could I eat as many sausages as I wanted, I was obviously having quite an effect on the ladies too. What a week this was turning out to be. It was only later that evening one of them explained that I was big news on the sausage front (ooh-er missus) and 'trend*ing*' on Twitter. Oh well, that'll have to do, I suppose.

Facebook can be useful to spread the word for all sorts of good causes, which is an upside of the new age. Mates tell me I should definitely become a tweeter as I've usually got a quirky opinion on something or other. The discipline of having to write whatever you want to say in 140 characters or less does make Twitterland a place where you can find real gems of pithy social comment and clever witticisms.

One of my mates texted last Christmas Day to say they had seen a tweet from the actor Simon Pegg, which did make me laugh. It read:

'Spare a thought for those working extra hard today. The Armed Forces, Police, Fire Service, Ambulance Crews, Noddy Holder's accountant ...'

Nice gag, Mr Pegg. I forwarded it to my 'people'. I thought they would appreciate it.

I do like having at least one good laugh a day, I do, I do.

*

The trouble is that the internet is everywhere: there is no escape. Access is available no matter where you are or what you are doing and people are not choosing to switch off from it, *ever*. I ask myself, do they call a halt in the middle of sex? I've lost count of the number of times someone has sat next to me in a cinema or theatre and started scrolling through their emails during a show. It's not just the young this addiction affects, it can be someone mature and responsible who should clearly know better. Everything soon will be virtual. We won't even need to use our hands to hold the device that is our lifeline. Google have already invented glasses to wear that will project internet images right in front of your face on a floating screen only you can see, the controls operated by waving your hands around in the air in front of you. There will soon be a robotic, goggle-wearing race talking into thin air with arms flailing wildly around as they surf the net, knocking bystanders out cold. It's not that far away, judging by how fast technology is moving forward. Just you wait.

If older generations find the latest technology irresistible, what on earth must it be like for the children of today who have never known anything else?

You tell a child that there was life without mobile phones and they find it incomprehensible. When I wanted to meet up with mates as a teenager you had to make an arrangement when you last saw them in the flesh, and then stick to it. Nobody on my council estate even had a phone in the house in those days. I was twenty-four before I had a phone installed. Unless you were where you said you were going to be at the time you had organized, that was it, moment gone, no chance of a quick call or text to change the plans. The same applied when arranging gigs and rehearsals with the band. The ability to get in touch with someone instantly means that forward planning, as far as youngsters are concerned, goes out of the window and everything is left to the last minute. So much for progress!

My generation's parents used to worry about the effect rock 'n' roll music would have on our development. Nowadays parents worry about how much their children use the internet and whether it is safe.

Is the time children spend in front of screens damaging to their health and their eyesight? I should think it probably isn't much worse for them than reading, or trying to tune in to Radio Luxembourg, by torchlight under the bedclothes was for me. In the fifties it was the only decent pop-music station crackling in and out from abroad. The real danger is *what* kids are reading and watching, not the way they are doing it. While I was secretly reading books like *Treasure Island* or *The Adventures of Huckleberry Finn* when I should have been sleeping, today's youngsters are able to look at websites devoted to bomb-making, self-harm and pornography.

Young minds are suggestible. There are images and information about horrific things that they would never usually come across in day-to-day life, but thanks to the worldwide web, those pictures and details can now be presented to them while they sit in the 'safety' of their bedrooms. Our children can be bombarded with material that is damaging to their confidence, emotions and mental health. I may not choose to join in the social media phenomenon, but I know not to let children have unrestricted access to a computer, out of sight of adults.

Incredibly, by 2030 depressive disorders are predicted to be the No. 1 health problem in the world and in the last ten years the number of children prescribed antidepressants in the UK rose by 70 per cent.

For those people who have a fixation on screens, a total emersion in a 'virtual' world and a lack of real interaction with family and friends mean those statistics must be more than just coincidence.

Children today appear to be under an enormous amount of pressure. Parents and the education system need to take responsibility for this. I've seen lots of examples where children are being pushed too hard both at school and at home and the only result is unhappiness for all concerned.

Schools are now so obsessed with league tables that competition is fierce and each school is desperate to produce a set of statistics that show they are achieving high grades in exam results. Exam results are all well and good but children can achieve many great things with not a GCSE to their name. Try explaining that to a youngster nowadays, mind you, and you won't get far. They are drilled into believing that A-levels and university are the only goals worth striving for, when in reality so many kids are just not suited to sixth form or studying for a degree.

So many university students complete three years of a course in all manner of subjects and emerge no nearer to deciding what they actually want to do. For those who are pushed into going to university by their teachers and parents because it is seen as the right thing to do, they risk a real chance of failing as it was the wrong choice in the first place. Result...unhappiness.

It is a firm belief that university is a rite of passage that everyone should experience, but I disagree. It does not suit all young people. There are other ways forward and you could just as easily be wasting those three years if you don't have a real desire to study a chosen subject. If someone wants to be a doctor, a lawyer, a teacher or suchlike, then qualifications are a necessary element, fair enough. If it's just a time-buying exercise while students figure out what they want to do, I don't think it has the same value. Teachers will have children believe a degree will lead to a more important, better paid job. Out here in the real world we know that isn't always the case. Anyway, it is possible these days to do a university degree later in life when you've already sampled a variety of jobs.

Similarly, some people would have you believe that an education isn't worth much unless you have paid for it…another theory that I simply don't accept. All of my kids went through the state school system. They achieved decent qualifications and all went on to further education. We may have been lucky that the schools they attended were good, but the kids all worked hard and had good encouragement at home. They all needed a 'kick up the backside' sometimes, like kids do, but I don't believe paying for their education would have served them any better. The schools they attended had all-round excellent standards and they took part in lots of extra-curricular activities that they not only enjoyed, but probably helped in the careers they eventually decided to follow.

In my day, learning was based all around the 'three R's' (that's Reading, wRiting, and aRithmetic). It's true there doesn't seem to be the same emphasis now, with text speak and spellchecking, so is grammar still relevant today? I'm of the old school – I can't send an email or a text unless every word is written fully and all correct punctuation is in place. This from a man whose song titles in the early seventies were phonetically spelt, were 'text speak' two decades before it became the norm and who got into trouble with the education authorities for doing so! I can see the irony.

It wasn't just the teaching methods that kept our noses in our books back in the fifties; it was partly the threat of corporal punishment. The strap and cane were in regular use at my senior school. My backside or the palm of my hand had red stripes a few times. Trouble was, if you went home and told your parents that you'd been given the cane you were just as likely to get another smack from your dad! Mums and dads didn't question school or police discipline methods as they do now. This was certainly a deterrent to misbehaving.

Children now are more aware than ever of their rights and demand respect from others without knowing how to give it back. Parents are often quick to complain about how their child is being disciplined without ever considering if it was little Jenny or Johnny who was really at fault.

When you look at what they are faced with, you do have to accept that teachers have a difficult time in today's society. The government constantly move the goalposts on what they want delivered and the pressure is always on to achieve top exam results. Schools need outstanding reports from Ofsted, the office for standards in education. Heads know when an inspection is due – an Ofsted inspector doesn't just appear without warning – and so setting up for this takes priority and on the day all is top-notch.

Not an accurate picture by any means. Like the Queen, Ofsted inspectors think the world is wonderfully tidy and always smells of fresh paint and disinfectant.

For some parents, a few qualifications are never going to be enough. The pressure at school can be intense but unrealistic expectations from parents can be even more overwhelming for youngsters. Middle-class parents are becoming more and more obsessed with being able to trumpet their child's achievements. Talk at the school gates and dinner parties can be dominated by a parent wanting to boast about multiple A* grades and how little Lucy is studying Mandarin Chinese and cello. We must not forget those attempting the fastest Facebook post on exam results day. Woe betide the child whose parent is desperate to tweet their record-breaking results, only to find a list of disappointing grades.

The latest craze is the desire to join the 'genius' club. Now, I'm not saying these kids who are being bragged about are not brilliant, bright and bursting with brains. I'm sure they are. A genius, however? I doubt it.

By the time he was twelve years old Wolfgang Amadeus Mozart had written three operas, six symphonies and a hundred other works. That's genius. As great as young Philomena is on the trumpet – Grade Six, you say? Wow! – it doesn't necessarily make her a genius.

It's also worth remembering the tale of child prodigy Sufiah Yusof, who was accepted into St Hilda's College,

Oxford, to study mathematics at the age of thirteen. A few years later she disappeared, only to be found working in an internet café, claiming her parents' constant pressure to be the best of the best had driven her to run away. Ten years after gaining her place at Oxford University she was found to be working…as a prostitute. A cautionary tale for any parent who thinks high achieving is a guarantee of success and happiness.

For the book *Gifted Lives*, written by Professor Joan Freeman, more than 210 child prodigies were studied. Of those 210, only six went on to be hugely successful adults.

All in all you're just another brick in the wall.

My missus has taught drama in primary schools for years and so I've seen many school productions. Everything from *Bugsy Malone*, *Jungle Book* and *Oliver!* to a rock 'n' roll version of *Romeo and Juliet* where Romeo was on crutches with a broken leg. (Don't ask! It's still a bit of sore point, not for Romeo, the broken bones healed well, but re-choreographing the dance sequences two hours before curtain up on opening night was a bit of a nightmare for Suzan.)

If you work with kids you have to take things like that in your stride and adapt to the unexpected. Suzan has had her share of random events – children refusing to wear certain costumes at the last minute, a boy whose voice broke just as he was singing his solo, parents demanding their child was cast in a particular role – but throughout it all she maintains it's the most rewarding thing she has ever done.

I understand why. She started running a drama club at a local primary school when she realized there wasn't any drama being taught there. A sign of the times. Her club was designed for just getting up and having a go – as long as you joined in you couldn't get it wrong. Getting up in a drama class to perform something, however small, can really build up a child's confidence and help them in lots of other areas of their life. The trick is to let them do it in their own time. Don't push them too fast, let them watch others and learn, and if it looks like fun they'll soon want to take part.

As soon as she started to work with the children it became obvious that they were gaining so much from the experience. Sometimes they'd join the club and be so shy they could hardly speak. Over time I watched those same children perform on stage in challenging parts such as Mr Bumble in *Oliver!* or the Wicked Witch of the West in *The Wizard of Oz*. The transformation could be incredible.

So often after a performance, parents of a child in the production would come up to me and tell me they were completely amazed at what Suzan had brought out of their own offspring on stage, completely out of character to what they were like at home.

I love spotting the future 'stars' in the chorus line, acting and dancing their socks off, just happy to be up there.

Football coach Justin Byrne could do with remembering that. He was in the media as the tyrant who ran a kids' football team for under-tens in Buckinghamshire. He made the papers after sending out an email to parents who questioned his rather harsh methods. Defending his right to leave some kids permanently on the bench and never give them a go on the pitch, he was quoted as saying: 'I am only interested in winning. I don't care about equal play time or any other communist view of sport.'

The kids on his team were under ten years old! Ridiculous. This situation is not unique by any means. My son was about eight when he began 'playing' for a little team on Saturday mornings. Although he was never going to be another Ronaldo, my lad just wanted a kick around, but for the first month he was allowed on the pitch for only about five minutes each game. Upset that he was sitting on the bench for an hour and twenty-five minutes every week, we had a not-so-quiet word with the 'coach', whose own son by the way, was on the pitch the whole game every week, even though he was useless.

Finally Django was brought on for the second half of a game. He played his heart out, scored twice and made a third goal. On the way home he was smiling but said he didn't want to go back and play for them again. He'd realized, even at his tender age, that he'd proved a point against the odds. How will you improve and develop skills at anything if you're not taking part? You may never score a goal at Wembley, but does that mean you can't contribute and achieve your own personal best? Of course it doesn't.

I hear inspiring stories from many wonderful young people on my travels, proving life is not all mapped out aged sixteen. During my reign as the 'King of Sizzle', I met a young woman who had made a drastic career change. This mum had got a little bored on maternity leave from her normal job, and with a baby to look after she decided to try and work from home. Setting up a smallholding and investing in a few pigs, she learned how to rear them, butcher them and make her own sausages. Within two years she was producing award-winning bangers, including one adapted from a recipe brought over by the Romans when they built Hadrian's Wall. Her story shows what can be achieved. There are positive people all over the nation working hard and taking pride in what they do. You get out of life what you put into it. 'Sausage-maker' may not have been her ultimate ambition when she was a girl, but she was happy, successful and, I tell you, those bangers were amongst the best I've ever tasted... Go, girl!

Don't let me give you the impression that I'm against moving forward and have a beef with the modern world. Not so. I just don't like the past being dismissed out of hand when it can still serve a useful purpose. Not everything is rubbish just because it's older, including me.

Where technology is concerned, you can be both embarrassed and have a laugh, even with something as simple as radio microphones and earpieces in TV and film studios. Sound engineers love leaving your mic turned on when you go to the toilet, so the whole control room can hear your private activity. On the other hand you can sometimes hear comments about yourself through an earpiece, when the mic in the control room has been left open. It can get interesting when the production team don't know you're listening in.

Sometimes, though, the old ways are the best, particularly when you are filming outdoors in a noisy and dangerous environment. Old-fashioned loud hailers still get used on film sets. I was doing a shoot for a frozen food advert in Scotland where I was a sea captain returning home after weeks trawling for fish. One really tricky scene had me climbing a ladder up the jetty with the rough sea below and the trawler passing behind me as background. It took a while to set up the shot as timing was critical, even more so considering the weather. We were using real fishermen on the trawler, who had been a hoot the day before out at sea. In their final passing shot all they had to do was wave goodbye at me, just as the director shouted 'Action!' through his loud hailer. The crucial cue came loud and clear, then out of the blue one jovial, hairy fisherman, through his own loud hailer, shouted back in his thick brogue, 'What's me motivation?'

It took me all my strength to hold on to the ladder. I don't know what it cost to retake the shot but the gag was worth it.

Chapter Six

NEW YORK, LONDON, PARIS, MUNICH . . . TALK ABOUT . . .

You do cover a lot of miles when you're in a rock 'n' roll band. You may already be aware that...

> *I've seen the yellow lights go down the Mississippi,*
> *I've seen the bridges of the world and they are for*
> *real.*

...Well spotted, Slade fans, those are indeed the opening lines to the song 'Far Far Away'. The lyrics also include '*the morning in the mountains of Alaska*', which references a fleeting visit to the remote Alaskan outpost of Anchorage. There's mention of the view of Paris from Montmartre and '*the hound dog singer's home*' is clearly a description of Elvis's mansion, Graceland, in Memphis. The line that always confuses people is '*arigato smiles stay in your memory for a while*', which is about Japanese custom, where '*arigato*' means 'thank you'. It's amazing how many people think I am singing about alligator smiles (though apparently you should never smile at a crocodile), so it's good to put the record straight. I've never had a close encounter with an alligator as far as I can remember but I have come across a few sharks in the music business over the years.

Anyway, it's a beautiful song, beautifully sung, even though I do say so myself, and not the only track that was inspired by my travels around the globe.

There was 'Forest Full of Needles', a song written after driving through the Canadian Rockies, where a forest fire had raged through thousands of acres of mountains. It just left burned tree stumps sticking out of the ground, mile after mile, as far as the eye could see, looking like a pin cushion. The whole area was decimated.

'Ooh La La in LA' is pretty self-explanatory with its references to Sunset Strip, the Sunset Marquee Hotel and American BLT sandwiches, '*enough to feed a horse*'...oh, those portions in the States. I was dreaming of a proper bacon sandwich, though, on a white bread bap, with brown sauce...ecstasy! Funny what you miss when you're away for a year or more.

Yeah, travel is great fodder for a writer but 'The Wheels Ain't Coming Down' was a song about one of the scarier aspects of jetting around the world, when the landing wheels on the plane literally wouldn't come down and we had to head off to San Francisco airport, where the runway is surrounded by sea, to prepare for a crash landing.

I wish I could tell you that was my one and only scary plane story. Unfortunately there've been lots, but I suppose as I've made over 5,000 plane journeys, odds are there would be some dodgy ones. Look away now if you are a nervous flier.

I was once in a plane that suddenly dropped from 35,000 to 3,000 feet, after losing pressure. Then there was the time we were trying to land in New York in the middle of a horrendous thunderstorm. Lightning bolts were ricocheting off the plane and the dozens of flights scheduled to land were refused permission. Instead, we all had to circle round and round, stacked up on top of one another. If you dared look out of the window you could see planes above and below while the storm raged around us. No one knew how long we would have to circle or how long the fuel would last.

Flights in small private planes can be pretty precarious if it's bad weather. We used to have to take a few chances if we were to make the next gig over a long distance and time was of the essence. I've been in six-seaters in rain-storms, snowstorms and gale-force winds. I've seen huge icicles hanging off the engines and the pilot having to wipe ice off the windscreen with his glove because of freezing conditions. There was not such sophisticated equipment in the old days and health and safety took a back seat. The priority was ... put on the show, whatever it takes.

It's all very well being a rock 'n' roller but no one wants to join the Buddy Holly, Otis Redding and Patsy Cline hall of fame in *that* way. You do get an insight into how the world lost so many of its music stars when so much touring in the USA was done in those small planes, back in the 1950s and 1960s.

One time, Slade hired a medium-sized prop plane to take us, some other bands and all the equipment and instruments to a festival out in Finland. It was easier than everybody doing the journey separately. We all boarded, took our seats, the equipment was strapped down and we began to pick up speed down the runway. Suddenly, just as we left the tarmac, there was a huge crash and the main door of the plane fell off, bouncing along the ground. The pilot turned the plane around, landed, and went back towards the hangar. Some guys quickly appeared, picked the door off the runway, nailed it back on, literally, to the gaping hole and off we went again!

I think we were all so stunned we were up in the air again before we knew what had happened. We found out later the plane was twenty-five years old and this was its last trip. It would have been ours too if we'd been at any higher altitude.

For all its pitfalls, the opportunity to travel to so many amazing places was a bonus for us working-class blokes. Nobody we knew in the very early days, unless they were in a band, had even been out of the UK. I've been lucky to see so much of the world, but there was not always enough time to experience places unless you had a day off. It's a cliché but it's true: on one-nighters you only ever see the airport, the inside of a tour bus or limo, the hotel room, the dressing room, then the gig itself and a club or bar afterwards to unwind. Then the pattern repeats the next day.

My time with the band meant I had twenty-five years of flying through so many airports, and checking in and out of thousands of hotels, that I've got travelling down to a fine art. There are some things I always make sure I do on every trip.

First, with the advent of so much airport security nowadays, you don't only have to think about what you've packed, but also what you wear. I always wear braces on my trousers, but the metal clips can set off the body scanner you have to walk through. So then I would have to suffer the humiliation of stripping off in front of hoards of giggling holidaymakers, while removing the offending braces, and putting myself in severe danger of having my trousers drop down when asked to raise my arms as the guards pat me all over. This mishap once revealed the novelty 'holly and mistletoe' boxers some wag thought I'd absolutely love as a Christmas present, and which completely destroyed any rock-god cred I may have had left.

So now I tie a scarf, hippy-style, through my belt loops to keep my trousers firmly in place. No metal buckle or clips and no danger of prying eyes seeing my underwear. (Sorry, girls!) It's a bohemian look I think I can carry off, especially when worn with the trusty straw hat I bought in the Bahamas for one shilling (that's old money) in 1968, a wee bit battered but still going strong…and you thought Sienna Miller was responsible for the Boho fashion craze. Get in line, girl!

In the old days touring with the band, many was the time airport security suspected we were long-haired louts trying to conceal something about our person that wasn't legal. We'd be whipped to one side and there'd be fingers up our arses before you could say 'personal use'.

I don't always go abroad when I fancy a break – there are plenty of places in the UK that I visit if I get the chance.

There's one particular hotel on the banks of a Scottish loch that's a great place for an escape. It's a fine castle with towers and turrets, and the view from the windows across the misty loch is sensational. Inside there are roaring log fires, stags' heads on the walls and tartan carpets underfoot. I do have to be careful my tartan trousers don't clash with the carpets! On arrival you are greeted by the hotel porters, always mature Scottish gentlemen dressed like Highland gillies, wearing kilts and sporrans. I may not be able to understand their accents sometimes (and they probably can't understand mine anyway) but they do know how to give a very warm welcome to Sassenachs. There is always shortbread and whisky on the bedside table but it never lasts long when I'm around. I've polished both off before Suzan has unpacked. She goes mad and I say, 'Well, you don't like whisky.' Her reply: 'But I do like shortbread.'

We took Django there when he was about twelve. He loved the place and couldn't wait to try some of the activities. He spent hours in the swimming pool that looks out across the water and almost as much time with his fishing rod out on the banks of the loch. The thing he was most desperate to try his hand at though, was archery. We booked him a session for one morning after breakfast. Once he'd had his porridge and I'd had my haggis and tattie scones with my full Scottish breakfast (I really must start a diet) we headed down to the archery field. As we neared the wooden building where they kept all the archery equipment we could see a couple of the gillies in heated conversation. I couldn't make out what they were saying but they were clearly agitated.

As we reached them, they turned and looked sadly at Django: 'Aye, we're sorry, laddie, there'll be no weapons for ye this morning ...'

We looked past them into the archery store and saw the place wrecked with just a couple of broken bits of wood where all the bows and arrows should have been.

There had been a break-in during the night and all the equipment stolen. The gillies were furious and were convinced some local youths must have been the culprits. They promised Django a free quad-biking session up in the hills to compensate for his missed archery lesson, but they also gave us a spine-chilling warning. Believing the local teenagers were now armed to the teeth, they told us to steer clear of the local town that night after dark.

'Ye best be warned,' they said. 'Stay in after y'dinner. There'll be a reet old battle raging on the streets of Balloch ta-neet!'

We took their advice and steered clear in case we ended up in some Scottish version of a Wild West show. Whatever went down in the local town, something must have happened, as we later heard that most of the archery equipment was back in place next day. You wouldn't argue with those gruff Scottish gillies!

That's not the sort of problem you're likely to come across in a city hotel. Staying in different hotels in different cities night after night when touring gives you a sixth sense about accommodation. First off: is the room I've been given the one I've booked? The right standard and size, with the view as described? No one is expecting the Hanging Gardens of Babylon or herds of wildebeest sweeping majestically across the plain from a Torquay bedroom window, Mr Fawlty, but if I've paid for a nice view then I expect to get one. Similarly I like a bathroom to include a bath, not just a shower. Otherwise, call it a shower room. As I get older and pickier, if my requirements are not properly met then I ask to move before I bother to unpack. In my misspent youth I'd lay my head down anywhere – and I've lain down in some very strange places indeed.

Another handy tip picked up on the road is to always pull back the covers of the bed and have a quick check that the sheets are fresh. No stray pubic hairs? You don't want a bed that's been used by the bellboy and the chambermaid for a bit of afternoon delight before you've checked in!

Don't get me started on 'boutique' hotel design. This is just a label for lack of storage space. You can get a big room with not even a drawer for your underwear. There are no hooks to hang anything on in the bathroom. They may have the latest power shower, whirlpool bath,

Jacuzzi and wet room, but you have to run the length of the bathroom naked and wet before you can get to the towel rail. Why? Minimalist, my arse! Style over substance more like.

Suzan and I were once upgraded to a fabulous hotel suite that was a favourite stopover for Beyoncé and Jay-Z. It had an enormous living room, dining room, three bathrooms, a walk-in sauna, massage and treatment room and a cinema! A recognizable face does come in useful sometimes! There was no need to step out on to the rainy streets: we ordered up room service and watched movies on the big screen. It was a really sexy room, all decorated in black and purple with low velvet sofas, big, plush floor cushions and lots of moody lighting. Only trouble was, it was all so moody and dark and the furniture so low on the ground that we were constantly bumping into and falling over things. I'm afraid I had forgotten to bring my night-vision goggles! Every time one of us tried to move around all we could hear was 'Ouch!…Ow!' and lots of swearing as one of us stubbed a toe. I wonder if Beyoncé and Jay-Z had the same difficulty. Maybe they employ a full-time assistant with a torch for such eventualities. Or both wear night-vision goggles. Kinky!

Room service is another way to distinguish a so-so hotel from a good one. In America, even roadside motels, off the beaten track, have perfectly good room service. The availability of food on offer, the fact it's served fast with hot food still hot, or cold food properly chilled, shows that it can be done. In Britain so many hotels seem to struggle with the concept of room service altogether. You can be paying good money in some large hotel but the staff act more like the old-style seaside landladies if you dare to return after half past ten and ask for food. It's a wonder they don't stand in front of you in their hair curlers wielding a rolling pin.

Recently, I checked in late at night in a perfectly decent hotel. Hungry, I asked for a cheese sandwich at around 11 p.m. in the busy hotel bar. I thought surely this couldn't be too difficult, but the trouble it caused. The night manager had to be called, as the barman refused to take responsibility for such an outlandish request. After much huffing and puffing they decided they *could* manage a cheese sandwich after all, but insisted I had to move to the hotel lobby to eat it in case it gave any of the other people in the bar any ideas and they tried to ask for food, too. Unbelievable. How do these places manage to make money? This wouldn't happen in the States. There you'd be served a huge filled sandwich with fries, potato chips, coleslaw and a gherkin on the side. Enough to feed you for a week and no problem. Lord knows what American tourists must think when they come over here.

Night porters do have an awful lot to contend with, mind you. I'd love to read a book written by one – it would be eye-opening, I'm sure.

Just last year I came back to my room in a hotel, late at night, and discovered a woman lying spark out in the corridor, right across my doorway. I wasn't sure at first if she was dead or alive. The only thing I was completely sure of was that she was stark naked. Not a stitch on her. What should I do? She was a real looker, gorgeous, but I didn't want to be manhandling her. Anyway, I didn't know where she'd been! To be honest, my first thought was that this might be some sort of candid camera set up, and if I started to try and lift her some paparazzi or TV crew might leap out and start taking pictures. So there I was, tentatively prodding at her with my foot to see if she was breathing, when she gave a sort of moan and wriggled about. I tried to wake her but she was out for the count. I couldn't just step over and leave her lying there and I didn't want to be discarding her in the corridor like a leftover breakfast tray. So I went back down to the hotel reception and got hold of the night porter. I thought the conversation might be a bit embarrassing.

'Um, there seems to be a naked woman unconscious on the floor in the corridor, outside my bedroom door ...'

He didn't even bat an eyelid. He just sighed and said: 'Show me.'

When we got to my floor she was still there, in an even wider, more revealing position than before. If I'd been a gentleman I would have been averting my eyes, but it's difficult, don't you think? Anyway, the porter just got out his pass key, opened up the door of the next room and grabbing the lady (I use the term loosely) by the ankle, dragged her inside.

Then he came out, nonchalantly closed the door behind him and said, 'Night, sir.'

I've mentioned flirting with the idea of moving to Paris in the past. It's one of my favourite cities in the world. I always knew I'd like it even before I went there and the reality did not disappoint. It lived up to all the artistic and romantic hype.

My first visit was in 1972 when I went there to perform at the famous Olympia Theatre. It was love at first sight. I was captivated by everything about the city, the style, architecture, art, fashion and the attitude. Parisians in those days had a reputation for being quite rude, especially to the English. They didn't disappoint with that either although I found if you attempted to speak a little of the language you could avert the worst of their disdain. That attitude has improved a lot in more recent years. They are still some of the craziest motorists on the planet, though. You attempt to drive around the Arc de

Triomphe at your peril: the drivers really do think they have '*carte blanche*' to do exactly as they want.

For me Paris has managed to maintain its belle époque charm from the turn of the nineteenth to twentieth century. The 'beautiful era' was a time of peace and prosperity when art and entertainment flourished, and Paris was full of cabarets, bistros and music halls. Look carefully enough today and alongside all the modern developments, tourist traps and fast-food chains you can still discover the Paris of old tucked into the side streets of Montmartre, Pigalle and the Left Bank.

There are still restaurants with dark wooden furniture and softly glowing art nouveau lamps where you seem to have stepped right into a painting by Toulouse-Lautrec.

When I first took Suzan to Paris, as she had never been before, she wanted to visit the Eiffel Tower. Perhaps she was thinking I would whisk her to the top, drop to one knee and propose. (I might add she hadn't known me very long at that point.) As we arrived at the tower she asked if we were going to go right to the very top. I'd been up there a few times over the years so was rather dismissive of the idea and said, 'What d'you wanna do that for? The view from there is exactly the same as from the first level, it's just that everything looks a lot smaller!' Oh, what a romantic fool I am!

Suzan and I chose Paris for our honeymoon and I took along a clipping of a newspaper review of an unusual restaurant. The place was basically someone's front room with half a dozen mismatched tables and chairs crammed in. We went on the first day of our trip to secure a table and had to wait a few days until we could get in for dinner. Underneath shelves full of knick-knacks and wonky pictures hanging on the walls, we were elbow to elbow with the people on the next table. Very 'cosy'. There wasn't much choice on the menu as the tiny kitchen and the one chef obviously couldn't cope with lots of dishes. It didn't matter. We had a typical French meal cooked to absolute perfection. French onion soup, beef bourguignon and crème caramel – all three were the best I'd ever had. F'kin' formidable!

After dinner we went walking the streets nearby, soaking up the atmosphere. We found ourselves in Pigalle, near to the home of the Moulin Rouge, the cabaret club with the famous red windmill on top. The area is a little bit rundown in places and has a reputation for its red-light district.

Ever since I made my first trips abroad as a teenager, playing through the night in raunchy German clubs, I've always had the inclination wherever I am in the world to search out, shall we say, the more nitty-gritty areas of cities. The jazz clubs and sleazy bars. You meet a much better class of person – well, certainly *interesting* characters – in these establishments. I've got friends in low places! I'll usually pinch a line from music hall comedian

Max Miller and say to Suzan, 'You're going to the dogs and I'm showing you the way!'

Nothing good happens after midnight, only bad!

During the day Pigalle is a great place to find vintage guitar shops hidden away in the side streets, but that night we came across a '*musée d'érotique*' (well, after all, I do come to Paris for the culture!). The large window had a tantalizing array of the sorts of delights that were on display inside. One particular contraption caught my eye. It looked like a commode with pedals attached to a wheel of stiff leather tongues. From the sign attached to it, and our limited French, we worked out that it was intended for a lady to sit upon with her feet on the pedals, and as she worked them the wheel would turn, causing the tongues to turn and stimulate the area between her legs at whatever speed was required. It had the appearance of a medieval sex toy and looked as though it had seen a lot of use. I've not come across any other versions of this device so I may apply for a patent. With a few modifications I can go straight into production. I think I'm on to a winner.

I'll walk for miles around Paris, there's so much to take in. My favourite area, Montmartre, is a bit of a climb uphill, but it is certainly worth the effort when you get there. At the highest point of the city is Sacré-Coeur, the impressive white stone church with its ornate domes making it look like an enormous wedding cake.

It's as breathtaking inside as it is on the outside, although nowadays they have very fierce security stopping visitors from using their cameras and mobile phones and videoing the services on their iPads. Why on earth would anyone want to do that?

One day Suzan and I decided to go inside every church we came across as we strolled through Paris, starting at the famous Notre Dame Cathedral. As we made our way around the cathedral we noticed a figure in a long, hooded cassock whispering and muttering to himself as he shuffled around. He wasn't doing any harm but he was a tad menacing and was clearly irritated at the presence of other people. We tried to keep out of his way but everywhere we went he seemed to be looming over our shoulders and getting a bit too close for comfort. Once outside we joked about the ghost of the Hunchback of Notre Dame and wondered if the character we'd just seen lived up in the bell tower and was also lovelorn for Esmeralda.

We carried on with our walk, wandering this way and that with no particular plan and came to the next church on our route. As we looked around inside, we couldn't believe it. There was the hooded figure again, still whispering and talking to himself and barging up and down the aisles of the church. He didn't seem to be looking at us and yet made a direct beeline for us. We looked at each other in disbelief. It was definitely the same guy, there was no mistaking him. How on earth he'd made it to the same church ahead of us I had no idea, although we probably hadn't taken a direct route. He got closer but his hood made it hard to get a good look at his face. We couldn't even make out what language he was muttering, probably some French dialect, but we weren't sure. Unbelievably it happened again at the next church we found. How could he be at this one as well? Were doppelgängers in every church? Spooky! We started imagining we had stumbled into some sort of *Da Vinci Code* scenario. It was all rather unnerving.

Stopping for some lunch we pored over the possibilities. Was it just a coincidence or had he followed us? In the end Suzan reasoned he may equally be thinking how odd it was that this strange British couple had been in the same churches he had visited that morning, and despite the fact there are dozens of churches in Paris, we decided that his church crawl had just overlapped ours.

After a bottle of wine between us, we struggled up the hill towards Montmartre and on to Sacré-Coeur as the final church destination of the day, joking all the time that the hooded figure would be following us.

We reached the basilica and took a good look around outside. No sign. Stepping out of the sunshine and through the vestibule, we stopped just inside and scanned up and down the aisles. As our eyes adjusted to the light, we saw that in the main body of the church there were many people seated on the pews in prayer, or wandering around, taking in the architecture. We couldn't see the hooded shape. Just at that moment Suzan was almost sent flying as this heap of sackcloth exploded through the door behind us and barged right into her. It was *him*! He was muttering even louder and was clearly more agitated than he had even been before. Sacré-Coeur was his finale obviously. He went straight past us and headed towards the altar of the church. We couldn't get out of there fast enough. We had no idea what or who he was but I was fairly certain he wasn't a Slade fan. We decided not to hang about and be sucked into a web of intrigue. I really must stop watching so many conspiracy movies.

We often holiday on the Algarve in Portugal and I find it a great place to relax and unwind. The people are friendly, the beaches and the fishing villages are so pretty and unspoiled, and the fresh fish is exceptional. We do seem to end up in scrapes regularly, though.

We once took a wrong turn driving around the medieval town of Silves and ended up as part of a funeral cortège for an hour and a half, with me bursting for a pee. My resulting language was not very respectful of the occasion, so the wife decided wisely to wind up the car windows.

Then there was the time that Suzan was electrocuted in a shop and blew all of the power out for the whole surrounding area when she moved a live cable connected to a lamp she wanted to buy. She looked like a cartoon with her hair frazzled and standing on end. Visibly shaken and a bit singed around the edges, she was luckily wearing her rubber flip-flops, which probably saved her life. While all this commotion and chaos was going on around us there was an impatient English lady in the shop pulling at my sleeve, saying, 'Can you just sign an autograph for my husband? He's your biggest fan and we are in a hurry.' Never one to let my public down I dutifully signed as Suzan stood with smoke billowing out of her ears. She was not amused.

Even more alarming was the day I nearly lost all the holiday money. I'd been counting out the euros I'd just bought, making nice neat piles of notes on the coffee table in the lounge of the apartment in which we were staying. Suzan came back from the supermarket and knocked on the front door, making me lose count of where I was up to. I opened the door to find her standing there, open-mouthed, gazing in horror over my shoulder. As I'd opened the door a gust of wind had blown in. All the cash was now flying around the room like a euro whirlwind and the through-draught was sending the notes out of the balcony windows. Heaven only knows what the people sitting around the pool below thought as it started raining money down on them from a clear blue sky. That Noddy Holder, crazy rock star, throwing his money off the balcony, trying to be flash.

I've been to New York many, many times, and in the mid-1970s I lived there for nearly two years. I love the place. There's nowhere else quite like it in the world. When I took Suzan for her first bite of the Big Apple we went over with my mate Swin and his partner Debbie. Swin was Slade's tour manager for many years and is a born-again New Yorker. He's from Wolverhampton but has spent recent years living and touring with New York-based bands so knows the city well.

We'd landed on St Patrick's Day in March deliberately. It's a huge deal in New York, with the Irish community there pulling out all the stops to celebrate. The weather the week before had been mild and very sunny so we were expecting a beautiful springtime trip, but wouldn't you know it, just as we landed it began snowing very heavily. It was so cold it knocked the very breath out of our lungs.

As soon as we touched down we could see Swin's transformation into a local take place and his Wolverhampton accent turned into Black Country Brooklynese. He ordered us to open our luggage there and then in the airport terminal and put on more layers of clothing. We did as we were told while he barged through the crowds, ordering airport staff around and getting our car sorted so we could drive into Manhattan in style.

He's a native New Yorker.

Driving into the city, visibility was poor: the snow was becoming a blizzard and it was pretty much a whiteout. So on her first time entering the city Suzan wasn't getting much of an idea of the vast scale of New York. The snow eased off and, freezing temperatures or not, we were determined to watch the St Patrick's Day Parade, so we headed into Manhattan. It must have been the snow covering the street signs that confused him but somehow Swin took a wrong turn and suddenly we found we were in a queue of traffic, but not just any queue of traffic. We had become part of the enormous St Patrick's Day Parade.

There were crowds lining the streets waving Irish flags and dancing leprechauns everywhere you looked. On the float directly in front of us Hillary Clinton was smiling and waving as we inched forwards. How we weren't hauled out of the parade and surrounded by FBI agents I have no idea, but Swin maintained his position that when in New York, you do as they do and act normal, as though you belong there. So we wound down the windows and waved to the crowds as we followed the former First Lady through Manhattan. I swear I heard someone say, 'Who's that on the float in front of Noddy Holder?'

We packed a lot into that short trip. Swin took us for breakfast the next morning to a backstreet dive with bullet holes in the windows. My favourite American breakfast, corned beef hash with poached egg on top, was phenomenal! One night we dined at an Italian restaurant in Little Italy that was reputedly a hangout for mafia mobsters. With its checked tablecloths and loaded platefuls of mouth-watering spaghetti and meatballs, it wasn't hard to imagine. With the music of Frank and Dino playing in the background I had to check the toilet cistern for hidden handguns!

The icing on the cake for me on that trip was managing to get tickets for a certain Broadway show. A production of *Cabaret* was playing at the old Studio 54, which used to be the hottest nightclub in New York back in the day. Now it was transformed into a perfect place to watch a show set in a 1930s Berlin cabaret club. The audience sat at little tables lit with deco-style lamps, sipping Manhattan cocktails. We felt we were actually inside *Cabaret*'s Kit Kat Klub itself.

Wilkommen ... Outside it is windy, but inside it is so hot.

The cold didn't let up for the whole trip, though we didn't let it spoil things. In fact, one night things actually got a little bit too hot. We were staying in a penthouse apartment at the top of a small hotel on the Upper West Side. Returning from a rowdy night out we were feeling a little tipsy and more than a little romantic. We lit candles and were relaxing on the sofa, watching some of the more bizarre TV channels available in New York. I'm not quite sure how she managed it, but one minute we were having a lovely, intimate experience; the next, Suzan had knocked over a candle on to my nether region, setting my pubic hair on fire. The smell of burnt hair filled the room and I was hopping from foot to foot and squealing. Suzan was no help. She was just laughing her head off and very nearly threw a glass of whisky over my private parts to douse the sparks, which would have made matters a darn sight worse. The next day Swin and Deb wanted to know why I was mincing rather than walking normally, so the whole story came out and I've never heard the end of it. Luckily no one on the sidewalks gave my rather feminine gait a second look. It's true what they say: in New York, anything goes!

Chapter Seven

FAME, REMEMBER MY NAME

The realization that I may be 'famous' hit me hard. So hard I looked like I'd been tortured, bruised all over and with the fingernails nearly torn from my hands.

It was 20 November 1971 and Slade were playing the Boston Gliderdrome in Lincolnshire, an old skating rink that held up to 5,000 people and a regular venue over the years for hundreds of musicians from the Beatles to Otis Redding to Jimi Hendrix. We'd been gigging practically every night since we formed the band in 1966, going down a storm in towns and cities the length and breadth of the country. But that night in Boston was like nothing else we had ever experienced before. Slade's second hit single, 'Coz I Luv You', had the week before knocked

Rod Stewart's 'Maggie May' off the top spot to become the band's first No. 1 on the charts. We'd sold half a million records in the first fortnight of release.

The atmosphere was off the scale as we walked on stage and even at our full-on volume we could hardly hear ourselves over the noise of cheering and screaming fans. We'd never had such a maniacal reaction from the opening song. The place really was jumping and the boyz were certainly going wild, wild, wild. It didn't stop there. The girls' screaming was ear-piercing, and suddenly a gang of them at the front of the stage totally lost control. Hands were reaching out and grabbing at me, clutching the fabric of my trousers and clawing their way up my legs. Being pulled back and forth, trying to stay upright on platform shoes and singing into the microphone, while still playing guitar, became impossible. I lost my balance, toppled back, banged my head on a cymbal and hit the carpeted stage hard. Next thing I knew the girls were pulling even more dementedly at my legs and dragging me off the stage.

Sounds like every young guy's dream, I know, but those teenagers knew no mercy and it was bloody painful, I can tell you. I desperately tried to keep myself out of their sharpened claws and dug my nails into the carpet, trying to anchor myself to safety. They were too strong for me. The rest of the band were pissing themselves laughing as my nails drew tramlines across the carpet pile. I was hauled into the jaws of the baying mob with girls all over me, hands grasping from all angles as each one made a frenzied bid for a clump of hair or clothing.

Our very bemused road crew were loving seeing me suffer and, *eventually*, came to my rescue. I managed to haul myself back on stage and carry on with the show. My clothes were torn to shreds and I was finding scratches and bruises for days. My poor beloved guitar had taken a bashing too and after the gig, somewhat dazed, I thought... 'So this must be fame.'

On that night in Boston the mid-1950s seemed so long ago. Then I was a kid standing in front of the bedroom mirror, in our terraced house in Walsall, pretending to be Elvis. I was shakin' the hips and using a broken tennis racket for a guitar. All I wanted was lots of music, money, sexy girls, a fancy car and fame!

You get to learn over a period of time that fame can have many different faces...

It can be amazing, rewarding, fickle, dangerous, addictive, cruel, long-lasting, fleeting, useful, notorious, scary, money making... I could go on and on.

But beware, fame is not for the faint-hearted. Fame can destroy you, as many have found to their cost.

When I was growing up I considered 'famous' people to be Hollywood film stars or American musicians. Their lives were a million miles from my normal day-to-day existence. You could hardly imagine Bette Davis, Greta Garbo, Bogart and Bacall or Frank Sinatra wandering around the local store or hanging their washing out to dry. Their level of global fame was not something that anyone ever expected to be able to achieve for themselves. Of course, you could dream of having mansions in Beverly Hills with chauffeured limousines and private jets. But this race was not human: they were beautiful aliens portrayed on a huge screen, as we looked on in amazement from the darkness of our cinema seats.

To us youngsters in a still grey, post-war 1950s Britain, all those stars appeared to be very grown up and sophisticated. All of the information about them was carefully controlled by their publicity machines. In the main you only saw and heard the things they wanted you to see and hear. In paparazzi shots the stars never looked dishevelled, they were always pristine, and all their 'romances' and private lives were carefully guarded or manoeuvred, so as to portray an image their studio bosses wanted you to believe.

Teenage movie stars did exist but they were rare. Judy Garland and Mickey Rooney were two of the most famous. They were seasoned pros by the time they hit puberty and had grown up acting, singing and performing. They weren't thrust into the spotlight without tried and tested skills, but both ended up with addictions due to the pressures of fame and a work schedule that never let up. It makes me laugh these days when young performers after one successful album or movie are already complaining and suffering from 'nervous exhaustion' and have to take time out. As our manager used to say to us in the early days, 'It's not the work that's knackering you out, it's the partying!' Harsh but partly true.

When Shirley Temple shot to fame at the age of five in 1934, in the film *Bright Eyes*, she had already been acting for two years. Most famous for her 'On the Good Ship Lollipop' routine, mums, dads, grandparents and children of all ages loved her, but as she grew up there was no route for her to follow in showbiz. What are the career options for a child star who is no longer a child? Shirley was talented, cute and adorable, with the ability to act and sing. This didn't help as she reached adulthood. Shirley's mother and father had squandered her fortune. She was the first true child star, known and loved all over the world, but Shirley retired from films in 1950, at the ripe old age of twenty-two.

In Britain the big stars of those days came up through the theatres and music halls, performing eight shows a week in every town across the country. These artists would hope to get on to radio and if they were lucky would cross over into films. This was before every home had a TV set, and so an act could tour for years without altering their routine because it hadn't been seen by millions already. Mix this in with a pantomime over the Christmas period and a long summer season at a seaside resort and you'd have a full year of work.

Forget Simon Cowell, this was the true test of a performer's metal.

Why am I bothering to hark back to that time when entertainers were treading the boards night after night? Well, my point is this...fame in those days could never be a case of overnight success. There was no *X Factor* or *Britain's Got Talent* to catapult you into the nation's consciousness. The characters who were my inspiration were on the wireless or at the local cinema or theatre and had honed their craft over years of performing. Not only were they practised and rehearsed within an inch of their lives, they understood their audience and knew how to keep even the rowdiest crowd entertained. They were versatile. More often than not, artists had more than one string to their bow. They might have been known for being a comedian but they could belt out a song or play an instrument. They might have been a talented singer, but had the ability to dance or chat to the audience and throw in a few jokes, should the occasion demand it.

I didn't realize it at the time but the famous people I grew up admiring had worked hard at what they did and learned to be the best they possibly could. Longevity was something everyone wanted and needed to attain. These were jobbing artists who had to keep working, making sure they stayed in demand and reinventing themselves when necessary.

I always wanted to be a thunderstorm rather than a raindrop.

I can't say I've ever been totally starstruck but it could have happened when Slade, still called by our original name, the N'Betweens, found ourselves recording in Abbey Road Studios in London. There were multicoloured Mini cars parked near the front entrance belonging to the band that were in the next door studio to ours. It was the Beatles putting down tracks for the *Sgt. Pepper* album. We didn't get to meet the most famous band in the world that day, but we did at least get to breathe the same air, hoping some of their magic would maybe rub off on us.

I did eventually get to meet up with the Beatles a few times over the years, except for John Lennon. He did come into our studio in New York one night after we'd finished recording for the day and our producer/manager Chas Chandler, who knew Lennon well, was on his own, mixing one of our tracks. Lennon said, 'I love this guy's voice, he sounds like me!' Best compliment I ever had...for my singing, anyway!

McCartney gets flak sometimes but I've always found him to be a smashing bloke. I should have interviewed him for a radio special not so long ago, but he came down with a bad throat on tour and so we had to cancel. His first wife Linda was charming and she could always remember where and when you last met her. It was Chas who originally introduced Paul to Linda at a Jimi Hendrix gig at the Bag o' Nails club in Soho. Who knows what it must be like to deal with the kind of fame that follows McCartney around every day? He is still the most famous musician and songwriter in the world after well over fifty years.

Real, everlasting worldwide fame is hard to come by. There was one memorable day in New York in the mid-1970s when I met three of the most famous people on the planet. In the morning I was in a hotel lobby standing at the reception desk, checking my mail. Suddenly all hell broke loose as a group of massive black guys came through the revolving doors. They were all solidly built, smartly dressed in dark suits and ties, all wearing sunglasses. They moved forward as one in a circle formation. The American onlookers were getting terribly excited and then I could see why. Towering above, in the centre of the circle, was the most famous man in the world at that time: Muhammad Ali. Gee-whizz, this guy looked mighty impressive. Big stature, impeccably dressed, beautiful just didn't cover it and with a beaming smile that lit up the room. I have to say he was the most handsome human being I had ever seen in the flesh.

Everyone was rushing forward to get a closer look and shake his hand. He was being obliging so I thought, 'I'm having some of this.' I've shaken a few boxers' hands in my time and their fists feel like they are made of concrete. Ali to me was *the* best ever Heavyweight Champion of the World and his huge grip was like an iron clamp even though he was exerting no pressure whatsoever. It is unimaginable to us mere mortals what it is like to be hit by such a boxer. Nor would I want to find out, mind you.

He floated like a butterfly and stung like a bee, but even Ali was not invincible.

Still exhilarated from that encounter, I was waiting for the 'elevator' to go up to my room. The elevator doors opened, I entered and pressed the button for my floor. Just as the doors were closing, in came a stocky black guy, again dressed in an expensive suit and shoes. He turned around and right away I recognized him. As the lift went upwards, I was facing probably the best player who had ever kicked a football into a net. It was the Brazilian, Pelé, who at the time was seeing out his illustrious career playing for the New York Cosmos. Soccer had never been a huge success in the USA but they'd brought in Pelé to promote the game. He had been at the very pinnacle of his sport.

Not wanting to let the moment go for the second time that day, I said to him, 'Thanks for all the entertaining football you've given me.' Yes, okay, I was fumbling for something to say quickly as there wasn't going to be much time. He thanked me and I followed up with, 'My name's Noddy Holder and I sing in a band called Slade.' Pelé replied, 'I know who you are, man. I really like your voice.' I'd forgotten we'd had big hits in South America before the days when you could go there and play live. Anyway, we reached my floor, I shook his hand (not quite as vice-like as Ali's but still a strong grip), out I got, the doors closed and he was gone. Was there a secret convention of the best world-famous sportsmen going on in the hotel that day? Who knows.

That was No. 2 on that day's meet marathon.

What a day this has been, what a rare mood I'm in.

So, it's evening, same NYC hotel, same lobby, and I'm standing talking to Slade's manager, Chas Chandler. Chas had discovered (in New York, by the way), managed and produced Jimi Hendrix. Before that he had been the bass player with the band The Animals, whose biggest hit was the classic 'The House of the Rising Sun'. Their records had been hits in the USA and, because of their music style, The Animals had met and become friends with many of the black soul and rhythm and blues acts in America. They were even present at Otis Redding's recording session of 'Dock of the Bay'. Jealous or what?

I digress yet again...so anyway, Chas, who was an out-and-out Geordie, had told us many times over the years that he used to date Diana Ross in the mid-sixties when she was in the Tamla Motown group, the Supremes. We would fall about laughing and wind him up with 'Fuck off, Chas, you never dated Diana Ross!' She was by now a huge solo star all around the world and...you've guessed what's coming, right? There's another commotion in the hotel lobby when in swoops the delectable Miss Ross with her large entourage. She spots Chas immediately, well, he was six feet six tall, and runs over and flings her arms around his neck, and with that recognizable voice says, 'Chas, I've not seen you for years and years, we used to have so much fun!' Chas was smirking at me from over her shoulder as he was hugging her and had a look that just said, 'Now I'll introduce you to one of my ex girlfriends!'

Strike No. 3 on Genuine Fame Day.

When I was young, to be 'celebrated' meant that you were being hailed for a talent or an achievement.

Nowadays fame as a 'celebrity' can be instant, but also much more fleeting. Appearances on a TV talent show or reality programme can bring a certain level of fame. It's usually backed up with coverage in tabloid newspapers and celebrity magazines with pictures of the new 'star' posing at home or giving us their fashion tips or favourite recipes. This is followed up with invitations to go on chat shows, where the person we are being sold as 'the next big thing' has their childhood or current love life picked over and examined in minute detail. Within a week there's nothing we don't know about them and we're tired of their backstory already. Never mind, there'll be another one along in a minute!

It's mostly young people who are catapulted into this fame game and often don't have any ability on which to hang their name.

On TV talent shows they at least have to perform to achieve the grand prize of a recording contract or a spot on a star-studded bill. They may have a great voice or the ability to perform as a dancer, comic or variety act. What the young ones haven't had the chance to do is gain experience. That comes from performing live in front of an audience and finding out what works and what doesn't. Building up a repertoire so there is a solid foundation on which to base a career is almost impossible if one minute you were singing into your hairbrush in your front room and the next you are centre stage in front of millions in

TV land, being judged not only by a panel of celebrities but by every armchair critic in the country.

You can *win* one of these shows and still be hurtled back to complete obscurity within a few months. I'd name names, but you probably wouldn't know who I was talking about! It can be just as traumatic for the families of these would-be superstars. Thinking they are going to bask in the glory of the millionaire lifestyle of their loved ones, and for it all to come tumbling down as quickly as it was built, can be distressing.

All performers have to develop a thick skin and the ability to cope with negative feedback and adverse publicity. It's all part of the job but not something anyone can learn overnight. The whole experience can be overwhelming and scary. Relentless attention for someone who is the slightest bit insecure can wreak havoc.

Fame… puts you there where things are hollow.

This is where my inbuilt self-confidence has always served me very well. I only ever get pissed off with critics if I agree with them!

Many people don't realize the amount of digital correction that goes on in images that appear in the media. Most of these airbrushed celebrities look good in the flesh anyway, but obviously not good enough for a world that demands perfection. Cascading locks and piercing blue eyes can all be computer-generated. Even the world's top models are slimmed down, have blemishes erased, curves enhanced or worse – completely removed. Many step beyond computer enhancement, and alter the real thing.

I've met many truly beautiful women over the years, and yet not one of them has been totally happy with the way they look. What hope is there for any woman if every 'famous' female they see in a magazine has had their cheekbones, tits and arses artificially lifted?

All I hope is that, male or female, you wise up and stop swallowing the myth that you can look 'perfect' with nips and tucks, implants and injections. All you do is look different, that's all, not perfect.

Liberal Democrat MP Jo Swinson conducted a parliamentary inquiry into body image. Her research shows that the current airbrushing culture leads to huge self-esteem problems in young people, and reveals that half of all sixteen to twenty-one-year-old women would consider cosmetic surgery. In addition, in the last fifteen years reports of eating disorders have doubled.

I understand the furore about the 'fakeness' of the images with which we're bombarded and I agree with the position taken by American writer and comedienne Tina Fey. She takes the line that better to be 'Photoshopped' than take a trip to the plastic surgery clinic, where the effects are much harder to undo, saying: 'At least with Photoshop you don't really have to alter your body. It's better than all these disgusting injectibles and implants. Isn't it better to have a computer do it to your picture than to have a doctor do it to your face?'

> *If you have a prune and you tighten the prune, you don't get a grape, you get a tight prune.*
> Tracy Mountford, Cosmetic Skin Clinic

Dissatisfaction with the way we look is not a new phenomenon or, indeed, one limited only to women. Portrait painters in Tudor times would enhance the best features of their subjects. Fashion itself has always been partly about enhancing or disguising whichever body part was in or out of vogue at that time.

Someone who did not need enhancing and who briefly wafted by me in LA, albeit when she was in her forties, was one of the most famous and stunning film stars ever, on and off screen, Elizabeth Taylor. Just as famous were her hypnotic lavender-blue eyes. Her uproarious marriages to Richard Burton, Welsh actor and renowned 'swordsman', and he of the dark brown voice, are well documented. When I was young they were *the* most famous Hollywood celebrity couple. They were obsessed with each other, but when two incredibly famous stars are married to one another it usually brings heartache.

Burton with a drink or ten inside him could be incredibly cruel, as I witnessed once in an after-hours drinking den in Soho, London. I was always the typical happy drunk, telling everyone around me 'I lurve you', but that afternoon a journalist friend of mine was on the receiving end of an undeserved tirade of intoxicated abuse from Burton. One minute he was a pussy cat and in the blink of an eye a roaring lion. I can't even remember what set him off, but it was not pretty, and I've seen the same thing happen to other heavy drinkers. I vowed I would never end up like that.

The Burtons' immense wealth was a good example of what can come with that level of celebrity. In the sixties alone they earned over $88 million and spent $65 million. They owned houses all over the world, Rolls-Royces, famous artworks and a yacht with fourteen bedrooms. They had a seventy-two piece set of matching luggage to carry their designer clothes, some never worn, in their private planes. They would book a whole floor when they stayed in hotels. Their lifestyle was unbelievable. Such were the trappings of fame.

Then, of course, there was an array of fabulously expensive and famous jewels that Elizabeth had to have. When they were out to dinner one night with friends, Elizabeth, in need of some affection, said to Richard, 'Hold my hand.'

Burton replied drunkenly, 'I do not wish to touch your hands. They are large, ugly and masculine.'

Famously, to make amends for this insult Burton bought Taylor a 69.42 carat Cartier diamond costing $1.1 million. The jewel was also being bid for by shipping tycoon Aristotle Onassis for former American First Lady Jackie Kennedy.

When Burton eventually presented the diamond to Elizabeth she commented, 'It will certainly make my ugly big hands less ugly!'

A couple of years later, seated next to the Queen's sister, Princess Margaret, at a dinner, Liz was flashing the enormous diamond. The Princess said to her, 'Is that the famous diamond? It's so large . . . how very vulgar!'

'Yeah,' said Liz. 'Ain't it great?'

Margaret, although a princess, was still a woman and couldn't resist any longer. 'Would you mind if I tried it on?' Liz slipped it on to the royal finger and Margaret's eyes sparkled.

Liz smiled and added, 'It doesn't look so vulgar now, does it?'

I love that story. You have to be seriously famous to come back at a member of the royal family like that.

In those days these were real stars, playing the fame game as if it was a movie. Nevertheless, with fame there's always a price to pay and the Burton-Taylor relationship finally ended very unhappily.

Another Hollywood star more famous for collecting endless diamonds, and nine husbands, than for her work (or maybe that *was* her work?) was Hungarian-born Zsa Zsa Gabor. On marrying yet another rich man she said, 'Darlink...what good is something hard on your finger when your man has gone soft, even after a double dose of Viagra?'

Hooray for Hollywood! Don't you just love it?

The really worrying stories are about women who feel so compelled to be seen in a certain way that they take risks with their health. Models have told me one trick they use is to eat tissues all day long, as they swell up in their stomachs and stop their hunger pangs. Some of the busiest models have been known to be regularly hospitalized as they simply do not eat enough to be healthy. One model was overheard at a fashion shoot claiming: 'It's my job not to eat.'

That *is* dangerous.

Couture fashion demands the thinnest of models for catwalk outfits. Apparently sample sizes of these garments are not even made in anything bigger than a size ten, yet most women in the UK are at least a size fourteen.

Former Australian *Vogue* editor Kirstie Clements became a whistleblower for the lengths models go to in her book *The Vogue Factor*. She revealed incidents like a model on a three-day shoot in Marrakesh eating nothing for the whole trip and claimed such things were commonplace.

She also described her attempts to move things along by featuring a 'plus-size' model, Robyn Lawley, a size fourteen. She knew the reader would appreciate seeing a more realistic representation of the female form, but her fashion department were harder to persuade and claimed nothing would fit or look good on such a large model. The shoot went ahead anyway and Clements revealed: 'When I went to the studio to watch the shoot most of the men in the room couldn't concentrate, she looked so sexy.'

Hear, hear! If the fashionistas ever asked a red-blooded male for his opinion on what looked good, I doubt the six-foot tall, size-zero brigade would get much of a look in.

Knowing they are in for intense scrutiny doesn't seem to stop the tidal wave of people willing to put themselves into the fame firing line. There are queues round the block to sign up for reality TV shows.

Those who don't audition for such things can still play the fame game in their own way. The desire to act as though they are 'famous' leads young people to treat their social media sites as a personal platform in their own version of a 'celebrity' lifestyle. How else do you explain the constant updates on their own movements, likes and dislikes, opinions and endless posing for pictures as though they are a starlet or ingénue in their very own TV show? They seem to believe they are at the centre of a not-to-be-missed, all-action movie!

Why do so many people cite 'fame' as the ambition they wish to achieve in itself? Why would anyone think that 'fame' by itself is the recipe for happiness?

There are certainly enough examples of the hazards of fame and recognition. The 'Twenty-seven Club' springs to mind. That's the list of musicians who succumbed to the excesses of the rock 'n' roll lifestyle at the tragically young age of twenty-seven. These icons, who should be remembered for their music more than for the way they died, include Brian Jones, Jim Morrison, Janis Joplin, Kurt Cobain and Amy Winehouse amongst others. The list covers a very wide period of time, proving, if nothing else, that while the world may change, the guarantee of a happy life once fame is achieved has never been certain. From James Dean to Sid Vicious, Marilyn Monroe to Elvis Presley, the stories of stars tortured and unhappy even after achieving the most amazing success are endless. Fame, for them, was clearly not the answer to all their problems.

Who knows how these people's lives would have turned out had they not achieved fame? They may well have had the same addictions to drink and drugs. In my experience drugs of any sort only ever enhance what is already going on inside you. For so many, it means that the panic and paranoia from which they are trying to escape are exacerbated and enhanced, which can have devastating consequences. Many creative people think drugs will expand their creativity, but it's pretty hard to be creative when you're dead!

The common perception of fame is that it is intrinsically linked to money, power and a privileged lifestyle.

That's the dream that attracts people to it. The belief that if you are famous you are treated better, have the best of everything and never have to worry about everyday life. It can happen like that...but rarely.

Money rather than fame brings freedom. Being able to say no to things you don't want to do, not being subject to the whims of others and to choose how you live your life are all easier if you have money. But you don't have to be famous to have wealth and fame certainly doesn't always bring money in its wake.

If the bubble bursts once you have achieved a level of fame and the work dries up it can be very hard. How do you go from being on a big TV show or in a popular band to trying to get a 'proper job' to make ends meet?

If anyone still believes 'fame' is a secret club they long to enter, I would point out that the trappings of a celebrity lifestyle are far more accessible now to people in all walks of life than ever before.

When a stretch limousine passes you in the street, it is far more likely to contain a gaggle of girls on a hen night than a film star sipping champagne on her way to a premiere. You are just as likely to be rubbing shoulders with networking business people in the Royal Enclosure at Ascot than you are a titled aristocrat, and the 'exclusive' cocktail bars and clubs that proclaim themselves 'VIP only' will let anyone in for the right price or if they look the part. And so they should!

Being famous doesn't always go with being critically acclaimed.

Are all the most famous people also the most talented ones? Discuss.

There are many examples of hugely popular and famous stars of stage and screen, in the music business and in all forms of creative media who sell vast amounts of product and are loved by millions, and yet they don't win awards or get hailed by the critics. How many times have you heard it said that J. K. Rowling is not that good a writer? She should worry! It must be annoying though, when you've penned the most successful series of children's stories ever, sold 400 million copies worldwide and become the first ever billionaire author.

It's ridiculous how often the most popular and successful forms of art are labelled of no value by snotty snobs! I've been the victim of that once or twice myself. 'You never have?' I hear you say. Yes, believe it or not I have! Musically with Slade we wrote and recorded happy, catchy, uplifting songs, which are the hardest to do. We did do some cracking ballads but generally we were 'party central'. Songs that are considered arty and worthwhile these days are generally a few minor chords strung together with the lyrics focusing on death, suicide and a slash-your-wrists attitude. The world is a better place than that, so why encourage youngsters that this is the direction we should be going in the so-called 'arts'? Get some balance sorted out. Let's make the world a happier place, not more doom-laden than it needs to be!

Spread sunshine all over the place...Just put on a happy face!

My good friend Brendan O'Carroll tends to suffer similarly at the hands of comedy snobs, and there's a lot of those about. Peter Kay and Michael McIntyre seem to get the same criticism.

Brendan is the Irish creator and star of *Mrs. Brown's Boys*, the top-rated BBC TV series with a succession of sold-out arena tours all over the world to its name. He and his wife Jenny are two of the most generous people I have ever met. *Mrs. Brown's Boys* was the most watched TV show on Christmas Day in 2013 with ten million fans tuning in to see the Irish matriarch and her loveable but dysfunctional family.

Brendan has not only created an enormously successful show, but is surrounded by a long-serving cast of family and friends who have performed alongside him in *Mrs. Brown* for many years. For much of that time they were struggling to survive, but now they have worldwide fame and are all sharing in the rewards for their loyalty.

When Brendan was signed to make his first TV series for the BBC, some of the powers that be in London wanted him to jettison some of the cast and crew who had toiled alongside him during the lean years. Brendan was having none of it and refused point-blank to even consider other people for the roles. He would have walked away from the opportunity rather than replace his loyal troupe. He got his way, and the folk you see performing alongside him are all 'family' in the O'Carroll world. Their camaraderie gives the show its warmth and heart on top of all the slapstick and side-splitting comedy.

The show has so far won two BAFTAs, two National Television Awards and counting plus an ever-growing clutch of others. Yet it wasn't even nominated at the most recent British Comedy Awards. As Mammy herself would say, 'Feck that!'

Brendan himself has a more considered response. He's a hugely talented and experienced writer, director, actor and comedian and has written five novels, two screenplays and seven plays, which he also directed and starred in before being catapulted to 'overnight success' with the TV series. The team have just released their first movie, which went straight to No. 1 at the box office.

In response to those who criticize his show, Brendan maintains: 'There'll always be a fucking donkey telling the racehorse how he's doing in the race.'

So, 'fame' – is it for you? Do you fancy a stab at it?

There's a lot to recommend it, I will admit, but I've done my best to give you an idea of just some of the perils.

Good luck...it's a celebrity jungle out there!

Chapter Eight

A NODDY IS NOT JUST FOR XMAS

'Iiiiiiiit's Chriiiiiiiissssssstmaaaaaassssss!' Come on, be honest, you've been desperate for me to do that since about Chapter Two. (If only I had a pound for every time someone asks me to shout that! Oh...hang on ...) Since 1973 I've become so associated with the festive season that apparently there are children nowadays who don't actually believe I really exist!

Luckily I feel suitably honoured to be considered an integral part of Christmas. It's a good job really because the whole shebang could drive me Christmas-crackers and completely brazil nuts. If all I did was bellow 'Bah humbug!' when faced with the holy trinity of tinsel, trifle and too much turkey, I don't expect it would go down too well. Having said that, I don't comply with every request to scream my most famous catchphrase wherever I may be.

It's not at all appropriate in a packed restaurant or the vegetable aisle of a supermarket. Come to think about it, it's pretty much inappropriate anywhere I'm normally asked to shout it. It does have a certain resonance in the gents toilet, but it has been known for the bathroom tiles to walk out on me! Somebody, somewhere, shouts it *at* me, at least once, every day of the year. Unlike Roy Wood, though, I don't wish it could be Christmas every day! Apologies if you are one of the many disappointed people who have tried to cajole me into roaring yuletide greetings, but there is a time and place for everything, and sitting on the beach on a hot summer's day, sipping a nice cocktail, isn't it.

Still, I'm really chuffed at having a big Christmas classic that has been going strong for more than forty years. Forty years! How is that even possible?

Funnily enough we recorded the track at the end of the summer of 1973 in a hot and humid New York. Not a festive atmosphere at all. I knew it was a catchy song, but it was not an easy task to record. We were in the studio only a couple of months after Don Powell, Slade's drummer, had been involved in an horrendous car crash that had killed his fiancée. Consequently, as well as all his physical injuries, he'd been left with no memory and no sense of taste or smell, and we didn't know if he'd ever be able to play drums again. It was a difficult time for us all to focus on happy music.

In Britain, December 1973 was the height of the 'Winter of Discontent'. All over the country there were strikes and three-day weeks. Money was tight and times were tough, everyone needed cheering up, and 'Merry Xmas Everybody' seemed to hit a nerve around the world and put a smile on people's faces. It was a rowdy record and I made sure, from out of the economic gloom, the lyrics were upbeat and optimistic.

Look to the future now, it's only just begun…

The record went straight to No. 1 in the charts the first day of release, where it stayed for five weeks, selling over a million in that first year. Even now I reckon it doesn't sound at all dated, and maybe that's what keeps it popular year after year. Well that, and the beautiful way it is sung…obviously!

Believe it or not I've had people say to me that they think I actually go around the country, as early as October, egging the stores on to play the record. What!? Anyway, despite the fact that I'm forced to do my Christmas shopping in June, to avoid the endless pointing at me while the song is playing in every store, I've always loved Christmas and I still do.

For me it is all about getting together with family and friends, having a wee drop of whisky, eating far too much lovely grub and nodding off in front of the TV. I expect it's pretty much the same round at your place.

It was just like that when I was a kid. Only with far less presents than most children get now.

My earliest Christmas memories are of waking up to find Santa Claus had left a small pillowcase at the end of my bed. It would have an orange and some nuts in the bottom, a bar of chocolate and a pack of playing cards or a set of jacks. Can you still get jacks? There were usually a couple of books, one always being an annual, *The Beano*, *The Dandy* or *Dan Dare*, or perhaps *Film Fun*.

It didn't take long to open up the gifts, not like today when some kids can still be opening them right through Boxing Day. I'd be thrilled with whatever I found and happily play for hours with a new box of tin soldiers, while my mum got stuck into making the dinner. I think she'd put the turkey in the oven in the middle of the night. You'd wake to the smell of cooking even at five o'clock on Christmas morning. I always wondered if Father Christmas stuck around to give her a hand with the sprouts, before he disappeared back up our chimney. In those days mums cooked vegetables for hours but they always seemed to taste great. How did that happen?

As well as the pillowcase, some years I might have an extra bigger present. This would depend whether my dad had money left over or not, although I didn't know this at the time. One year I got a train set. Nothing complicated, just something that went round and round on a circular track. My dad knew I'd spent hours looking at a model railway layout that was always on display in the window of our local general store. It had proper bridges and tunnels, but I loved my own little version, and I made my tunnel and a station out of old shoe boxes. In the centre of the track was a make-believe field with tin cows and sheep playing happily alongside a lion, tiger and giraffe.

Another year my Uncle Eric made me my very own puppet theatre. It had red curtains and came with various hand puppets. I used to set it up in the yard at the back of our terraced house and all the kids from the street would come along. Admission charge was one old penny but they'd get their money's worth even in those days, and I'd entertain my audience with a Punch and Judy show. I knew the plot from watching the real Punch and Judy shows on daytrips to the seaside but there was only room for one puppet master behind the curtain so I would switch between being Mr Punch, poor Judy, the angry policeman and the scary crocodile. That's the way to do it!

I'll always remember the year I got a full cowboy outfit. I must have been five years old. I was mad about Hopalong Cassidy and the Lone Ranger, having seen them at the Saturday morning cinema shows and later on TV. Hopalong Cassidy, played by William Boyd, broke the tradition of the 'good guy' always wearing the white Stetson. He wore a black one, which was customary for the villain. This stemmed from the original books in the early 1900s, when Hopalong was written as not a very nice character. His image was changed for the movies. Luckily I got the black cowboy hat, 'Yeeee haaaarrh!' All the girls love a bad boy. I also got a plastic sheriff's badge and spurs, and a holster with two cap-firing guns. I could swagger through the streets of Walsall keeping an eye out for outlaws or be riding out on a horse in a star-spangled rodeo.

*On the road to my horizon, but I'm gonna be where
the lights are shining on me.*

Christmas dinners then would be much the same as I dish up at home these days, except my veggies are a bit more *al dente* than my mum's were. Roast turkey and all the trimmings and no fancy starter, you just got stuck straight into the main event. Back then, though, we'd leave enough room for my mum's homemade Christmas pudding and custard. Yes, it definitely had to be custard in those days.

Also, there'd be no lounging around in pyjamas all day, like my family love to do now. We'd be wearing our best clothes, all topped off with a wonky paper crown from a cracker. I've just thought, maybe everyone made the effort to be smart because we'd be in the presence of the King, or in later years the Queen, when everyone in the country sat down at 3 p.m. to listen to the Christmas speech.

Relatives in working-class families often used to live within walking distance, or at most a short bus ride away, from one another. Even if snow was thick on the ground, and it usually was, you could just wrap up and trudge through it to get to each other's houses. These days, with relatives sometimes scattered all over the world, a big hassle at Christmas are the horrendous journeys people undertake to make sure they see as many of their loved ones as possible. Delayed air flights, overcrowded trains and hours spent on motorways stuck in traffic jams were never part of my Christmas as a kid. In fact, motorways hadn't even been invented when I was a kid!

With Slade, we did make a point of travelling through the night from wherever we played on Christmas Eve so we could get home to our families. By the time we set off after the gig roads would be pretty empty so it would just be a case of trying to beat Santa's sleigh and get home before the kids were awake and opening their presents. Many a time on those merry journeys I've spotted something suspicious, a flash of red and white, zooming overhead.

*

There has been the odd occasion, in recent years, when my family have decided to go to a restaurant for Christmas lunch, just for a change (no casting of aspersions on my cooking, by the way). We know this is taking our lives in our hands, as inevitably Slade's Christmas song will come on in the background alongside all the other festive faves, and the other diners will fully expect a singalong-a-Noddy. Now, I'm used to this happening after so many years – let's just call it an occupational hazard – and I do join in the fun.

One year things went a bit too far. A couple sitting on the table next to ours got talking to us, and the fella told me he managed bands. He asked if he could give me a demo recording of one of his acts for me to listen to and give an opinion. I do get this a lot and I said I would give it a listen. The next thing I know, the guy had gone and told the owner of the restaurant that I wanted to hear his CD immediately, over the dining-room speakers. This cacophony of thrash metal noise came out full blast and it was me who got the blame from the other families who'd been enjoying their Christmas meal up to that point. This guy had purposely booked himself a table next to mine and, after we got the ear-bashing sound turned off, he had the cheek to ask me what I thought of the songs. My answer is unprintable.

*

Christmas and Boxing Day, when I was a youngster, would be like Groundhog Day. You could pretty much set your watch by what you'd be doing at the exact same time, year after year. The party favourites, the tipsy sing-songs, granny showing her long knickers after a few too many sherries or snowballs (ask your gran!). For a kid that was comforting and the familiarity made it special. My mum and dad put so much effort into making it a magical time for us all. What I wouldn't give to have one more Christmas with them.

The death of my father, in 1988, hit me hard. I'd never known either of my grandads as they had both died long before I was born. One grandma died when I was very young, and the other while I was away on tour in America and I wasn't able to get back home to see her one last time. So the loss of my father was the first time I'd had to deal with a death of a close family member first hand. He had not been well for some time and it was agonizing watching him get weaker and weaker, in terrible pain and wasting away. Please somebody shoot me if I get to that stage. I don't want to put my nearest and dearest through the trauma.

At the time all I was hearing repeatedly from everyone around me was, 'When are you going back on the road with Slade?' 'Fuck off, I'm not' was the stern reply. There was a lot more important stuff to be dealt with in my life. Why couldn't people give me a break? I'd been working with Slade at that point for twenty years and with other bands before that. Some folk think you're a robot, have no feelings and are only there to please them.

I'd been taking my mum from her home in Walsall to visit Dad at the hospital, twice a day for months. He was getting no better and all the doctors could say was, 'It's only a matter of time.' I thought I had prepared myself for the inevitable, but when it finally happened it was like being hit with a sledgehammer.

We were in the ward at the end of visiting time, just before 3 p.m. one afternoon, and the bell to leave rang out around the building. My mum bent down to kiss Dad goodbye and I bent over him to do the same. His voice had been getting gradually quieter for a while and by now it was hard to decipher what he was saying. He was mouthing words and pulled at my shirt collar so that my ear was next to his mouth. He'd somehow rallied the strength to do this, as for weeks he couldn't raise an arm. He whispered a few private words to me, which I thought were strange at the time. I mentioned nothing to my mother as she was always upset enough leaving his bedside. Like any couple, they'd had their ups and downs but they'd been married forty-nine years, one year short of their golden wedding anniversary.

My dad had always been the life and soul of the party and his favourite party piece, after much beer, would be to sing Al Jolson's version of 'You Made Me Love You' to my mum. For their generation it was unusual to openly display affection in front of other people, certainly as they got older, and these performances were the only times I ever saw him do it in public. Everyone would roar with laughter as Mum would act suitably coy at his rendition, as if they had just met and not even kissed. I would joke with the family on these occasions that I must have been an 'immaculate conception'.

So this afternoon we got back home to Mum's house after the hospital. We were taking off our coats and I pointed out to Mum that the old wind-up art deco clock, that had always stood on the sideboard in the living room had stopped, with the fingers pointing at three minutes past 3 p.m. Mum gave it a tap to see if she could get it ticking. I'd never known this clock to lose time, and it always chimed every hour, on the hour. Just then the phone rang. It was a nurse at the hospital telling us we needed to go straight back, as my dad had died just a couple of minutes after we'd left his bedside. This was a week short of Dad's seventy-eighth birthday.

That clock never worked again but it remained on the sideboard in Mum's front room, where it belonged, and the fingers stayed at three minutes past three.

When I went to see my dad laid out in his coffin in the little Chapel of Rest, he looked twenty years younger. All that pain and suffering had melted away. It's true what Hamlet said in tribute to his father: 'He was a man, take him for all in all, I shall not look upon his like again.'

Mum and I cried together over the next few days, but once the funeral was over we dealt with that empty chair each in our own way. I never realized how the aftermath of losing my dad would rip out my insides, even after the initial shock was out of the way.

> *No man is ever a real man until he has seen his father buried.*
>
> African proverb

My mum, then aged seventy-three, would be living on her own for the first time ever. She never cried over Dad in front of me again, and was adamant that she would not move out of her home to be nearer to me, and I couldn't blame her. Most of her friends lived near, and I was mostly in the country now if she needed me urgently.

The death of my father brought home to me more than ever how much I'd missed out on in the past, family wise, with being away so much. It was the life I'd chosen and a life I enjoyed, but it reminded me again that I had missed seeing Charisse and Jessie in their school plays and concerts. It doesn't matter if you know the kids or not, a school nativity play can always bring a tear to your eye . . . or give you a good laugh! Especially if they're bursting for the toilet. Bless 'em.

I read an article once that said you could tell a lot about a person from the part they played in their infant nativity play. Interesting. I wouldn't have thought I'd be first choice for the Angel Gabriel, would you?

During my first year at school, Mum had to fashion a complete Angel Gabriel costume when I was cast in the role. A long white robe, some feathery wings and a tinsel halo slightly askew. I've never been able to keep my halo straight for some reason. This ensemble linked to my suitably angelic expression gave me my first taste of life on stage. I put my all into delivering my biggest line to the cowering shepherds: 'Do not be afraid, I bring you good tidings of great joy.' Technically speaking, I think the Angel Gabriel only visits Mary to tell her she will have a baby. It's a totally different angel who appears to the shepherds. My teachers weren't particularly worried about the finer points of the story, and as one angel looks pretty much like another, I think the Angel Gabriel is often asked to double up in this role. Where is Equity, the actor's union, when you need them?

There was one other time I had to wear a costume as part of a nativity scenario. A pal of mine decided to have a fancy-dress party coming up to Christmas. I suggested it would be a laugh to cast all his guests as characters from the nativity story and we each had to come dressed accordingly. I copped for the role of Joseph this time, as my mate thought the Angel Gabriel was stretching it a bit too far at my age and not appropriate after the things I've got up to in my time. So there I was with a tea towel tied on my head, sackcloth tunic, sandals and a tool belt (well, Joseph was a carpenter).

We were all having a fine old time, getting into the true spirit of Christmas. I'd planned to drive myself home later, so I had one beer then stayed on soft drinks the rest of the night. I'd got a very early start working on a TV show the next morning.

Around midnight it was time to make a move so I bid my farewells, and said I'd be heading for the Star in the East. I was feeling a little flushed just before I left, but I thought as soon as I got into the fresh air it would clear.

So I was in my car driving home and this strange feeling started to circulate my brain. I'd had the same feeling way back in the seventies. Then, some idiot in a Spanish bar had slipped a tab of acid into my drink without me knowing. It was happening again: I was hallucinating. I had to carry on heading home, I'd got no choice. I was driving really slowly through the town and finally came out on to an open road with twinkling purple lights all around me. Suddenly, out of the blue, I had to ram my brakes on. In my main headlight beam, right there in the middle of the road, stood a donkey. Well, was it a donkey? It looked like a donkey, it was staring at me with a face like a donkey, but, it was a multicoloured donkey! Or was it …

Just an illusion?

I'm sitting there, off my face and trying to focus, wondering what to do next. I couldn't manoeuvre the car around the animal as there was not enough space. Do I just drive straight ahead as there could be nothing at all there? I decided I had to get out of the car and check. I walked forward – don't forget now, I am tripping the light fantastic – and put my hand out slowly to stroke the apparition's body. Ooh yes, it was real, sure enough. What do I do now? I've got to try and coax this critter off the road so that I could get the car past. There was a length of chewed soggy rope hanging from the donkey's neck that felt like stretchy plasticine. I was tugging hard, trying to pull the stubborn creature over to the grass verge. He, or she, was having none of it. The silly ass would not budge. I would have to try a different approach, pushing from behind. Both palms of my hands are on the donkey's buttocks, I'm heaving and cursing like mad, and wouldn't you just know it, at that moment, along the road came a flashing blue light, stuck on top of a police car.

'Well, well, well…what have we got here?' Two coppers came over, highly amused at the fact they have come across Noddy Holder, just before Christmas, dressed as

Joseph of Nazareth, in the middle of the night, pushing a donkey. What more could they have wanted? It was a fair cop made in heaven.

The state I was in, there was only one line I could come up with...'I've left Mary in the stable with baby Jesus, the shepherds and the three wise men. I'm on my way to have a drink to celebrate the birth!'

'We've heard it all now. Get going before we nick ya!'

There was no mention of my slurring or glassy eyes so maybe they were in a 'goodwill to all men' kinda mood. So off I sailed into space with a green sea all around me.

> *Rebellion hasn't left me. Like sex, it just takes me longer to get going.*

Of course, there's only one way to ensure I'll always be King of Christmas, the font of everything festive and the know-it-all yule meistersinger, and that's to remain as Santa's chief deputy. I've stood in for him on many occasions over the years, and he still calls me up on Christmas Eve to help out with the deliveries if he's running late. Keep your eyes peeled, as you never know when it's the main man in the oversized red outfit... or me! If I take over to give out presents to kiddies at charity Christmas parties, I do have my own distinctive style that might give me away. I don't ask the kids (or sometimes it could be adults) if they've been good all year. Oh, no! I ask them to cough up and tell me if they've been bad, and what *naughty* things they've done. Oh, the confessions I've heard! It's hilarious how honest kids will be if they think the gift they are about to receive depends on it.

My favourite place to be Father Christmas is at the Children's Adventure Farm in Cheshire. I'm a patron of the charity the Children's Adventure Farm Trust (CAFT). They do an amazing job giving holidays and fun days out to children who are terminally ill, disabled or disadvantaged. Some of these kids have never had a Christmas present ever. Imagine that, in this day and age. It's a real eye-opener and often a tear-jerker.

Every Christmas CAFT build a fabulous grotto covered in fairy lights, with a throne for Santa and real reindeer. Then every day for the six weeks before Christmas, a bunch of kids are invited for Christmas lunch. They play games and then each of them gets a customized bag of goodies from Santa. They have a different volunteer Santa every day.

The kids come into the grotto one by one but sometimes they can be a bit nervous, so their carers hold their hands and bit by bit they edge closer and closer. I'll take the mickey out of their teachers and nurses by asking if they themselves have been naughty that year! The kids love it and even if they can't speak well they have a laugh when I tease the grown-ups.

Last year a boisterous lad came charging into the grotto and he certainly didn't hover in the doorway, but galloped around the room whooping and shouting. I let him burn off some energy and then asked him what he was doing. 'Gannang,' he shouted.

'Sorry, what was that?'

'Gannang, gannang, gannang!' he exclaimed louder and louder.

It took a moment but we realized he was saying 'Gangnam', like the song. The way he was charging about was his version of the 'Gangnam-style' dance, the one that looks like you are simultaneously wielding a lasso while riding a horse. His version was more like a bucking bronco. The CAFT charity workers, who double up as elves in the grotto, spotted a comical opportunity. One asked the lad, 'Ooh, Santa has always wanted to learn how to do "Gangnam-style", can you teach him?'

This was an extra gift for him. Soon he had me galloping around the grotto after him, and minutes later we both erupted through the door to the cheers of all the waiting children who thought it was hilarious to see a bearded man in a big red suit throwing some serious shapes. Santa's stuntman has still got it!

And I've still got all the credentials to carry on as Mr Claus' main stand-in. Deep throaty chuckle, check. I can easily switch from 'Baby, baby, baby' to 'Ho, ho, ho', no problem. Twinkly eyes and a cheerful disposition, check. I've even been working very hard on my round little belly... that shakes when I laugh like a bowl full of jelly!

Christmas for me now is always a mixture of emotions. It's a joy when little children come and tell me they've just sung our Christmas song in the school concert. On the other hand it's sad when you realize how easily a life can turn upside down. I try to help out Street Smart every year, a national charity raising money for the homeless. One day each year, John, the owner of Choice Restaurant in Manchester, puts on a full Christmas meal for as many homeless people as he can. I have helped out as a waiter on occasion, and when you get chatting you find out they come from all walks of life. Rich or poor, whatever religion or nationality, healthy or ill, they all have a heart-breaking story to tell.

I appeared at a carol concert, in aid of the NSPCC, in Manchester Cathedral about three years ago. I read out the poem 'Twas The Night Before Christmas' and it went down really well. This prompted me to accept an offer to appear at Union Chapel in north London to narrate a new take on Charles Dickens's *A Christmas Carol*. This venue was the perfect setting for the story, which we adapted around the music industry, with Scrooge becoming a record company boss. I was cast to play all the roles, and we had a merry band of musicians doing acoustic versions of unusual Christmas songs interspersed into the narrative. These are the kind of challenges that get my rocks off these days, something that comes entirely from leftfield and I've never attempted before.

Funnily enough, there is one obvious thing that I've only ever been offered once, and that is pantomime. I was already working so had to turn it down. Panto can get frowned upon by the snobs, but it is usually the first experience kids have of live theatre. Brian Conley and Joe Pasquale are two doyens of British pantomime. When he was younger, Django was eager to see Joe as Smee in *Peter Pan*, so we went along to the final matinee performance of his long run. Now, as we all know, Joe has a trademark, very high-pitched voice. He invited us backstage after the show and was showing Django how all the magical scenery worked. We ended up in Joe's dressing room and, as he'd got the evening performance to do in two hours, he had a machine on the go that kept his throat lubricated. It was just like being in a steam room, and Django said to Joe, 'Is this what makes your voice so squeaky?' Joe loved it! You couldn't make it up.

Christmas Eve 2002 is a date that will be forever etched in my memory. A few days before, my wife had driven my mum to our house for the festive season. Mum was feeling a little under the weather and we put it down to her age, eighty-seven, and the winter climate. The night of 23 December all the family went to bed as normal. Usually, when she stayed with us, Mum would be first up at 6 a.m., making herself a cup of tea and pottering about in the kitchen. When Suzan went downstairs around 7.30 a.m. on Christmas Eve morning, the lights were all on but there was no sound. She went into the lounge to find Mum, head bent forward, asleep in her armchair. Suzan tried to prop her up and make her more comfortable but there was no movement.

She ran upstairs and woke me up with 'You've got to go downstairs right now, I think your mum is dead in the armchair!'

I was still half-asleep. 'What did you say? You'd better be sure, coming out with something like that.'

Suzan was filling up... 'But I don't know what it's like. I've never seen a dead person before.'

I rushed down and found my mum had passed away gently, with me and her family near, just as she would have wanted it. It was as if she had been hanging on until she was under the same roof as us. Seeing as it didn't happen in her own home, we had to first call our doctor, then the paramedics had to come, then the police were summoned to make sure we hadn't bumped her off, and finally the undertakers. Don't forget, this was Christmas Eve so the medical services were not all working as normal. It was chaos and Mum would not have wanted all this attention.

We had an added problem in that we didn't want to tell my son Django right away. He was devoted to his grandma and she to him. As he was only seven years old at the time, Mum would not have wanted his Christmas spoiled. We managed to get one of our friends to take him out for the day, telling him Nanny had to go to hospital for a few days. You could see in his face he knew that it was something more serious. The whole family managed to get through Christmas on adrenalin alone, and we made it a celebration of her life rather than mourning her death.

We couldn't make any arrangements for the funeral because of Christmas and New Year and everywhere was closed for ten days. We would need to have her taken back to the Midlands but I couldn't register the death because there had to be a post-mortem. It was one hurdle after another, on top of the stress.

Then the day finally came when I would have to face going down to her house. I walked in the door and a lingering faint smell of her perfume was in the air. Julie, her fantastic carer, was waiting for me. She was really upset, as she had looked after my mum for years. Julie said the last time she saw my mum, two weeks before, she somehow knew from the way she spoke that was a final goodbye.

Before I started checking around, Julie told me she had strict instructions that if anything ever happened, and before I did anything else, I must open an old rusty Quality Street toffee tin that I'd seen displayed on the lid of her piano for a decade at least. I'd always assumed that it contained just household paperwork, insurance, her pension book, stuff like that. I opened the tin and it was stuffed full of letters, all neatly stored and still in their envelopes. I carefully opened the top one, then a couple of others. They were all love letters, perfectly preserved, that my dad had written to her when they were young and while he was overseas during the Second World War. Incredible. This was the moment the floodgates opened and I just broke down and sobbed. It was the release I needed: they were going to meet up again.

Back to that stopped clock on the sideboard. It was the day of Mum's funeral and I was outside her house guiding family and friends inside to the lounge. I was also helping lay out on the lawn the many floral tributes that folk had kindly sent. Lots of the neighbours I'd known for years were waiting for the send-off.

On time, the hearse carrying Mum in her coffin was coming down the hill and pulled up at the path to her front door. Everyone inside the house was shouting, 'Noddy...she's here, she's here!'

I ran in with 'I know... I've been outside... the hearse has just pulled up and they are loading the flowers.'

One of my relatives said, 'No, no... we didn't know the hearse had arrived. It's the clock, it's been chiming for about a minute!'

It was the first time the old clock had made a sound since my dad died, 15 years before.

Mum still comes to visit us at home nearly every Christmas. We get a whiff of her perfume, and sometimes there is a light silvery trail along the carpet from the armchair where she died through to the door where she left the house for the last time. Spooky!

Happiness is like a butterfly which, when pursued, is always beyond our grasp, but if you sit down quietly, may alight upon you.

Nathaniel Hawthorne

Chapter Nine

IF I RULED
THE WORLD...

In this book, I've given forth my opinions on everything from fashion to Facebook, so now let's make things really interesting and take things just a little step further. How about envisioning a world where I'm in charge and the laws and policies governing the land are all from the Holder manifesto?

You may scoff, but most of the population laughed at The Official Monster Raving Loony Party (OMRLP) when it started. Well, they still laugh when you get some bloke dressed like an Eskimo gurning over the shoulder of a Conservative candidate at a by-election count in Canterbury. Did you know lots of OMRLP policies, at which people once sniggered, have become laws over the years? The founder of the party, Screaming Lord Sutch, had a rock 'n' roll background and in his first foray into politics as the National Teenage Party, in the sixties, he campaigned for the voting age to be lowered from twenty-one to eighteen. Not a bad start for a 'joke' party.

The OMRLP manifesto is full of proposals that seem completely unworkable or too absurd to even consider, but they always have a point. Often it's to highlight what they consider to be real-life absurdities, and let's face it, there's a hell of a lot of those about and someone needs to expose them. Along the way, they have championed issues we now incorporate into our daily lives – free family planning, passports for pets, all-day pub opening, licensing for commercial radio and the abolition of the 11-plus entrance exam for children are just a few. They led the way in exposing the scandal of butter and milk surpluses being dumped down mine shafts. This had been sanctioned under European Community rules to maintain prices. Bringing this outrage into the open resulted in the redistribution of these foodstuffs to charities and people in need. Okay, it was also suggested the butter mountain be turned into a ski slope for Eddie the Eagle, but this bonkers statement brought a ridiculous waste of food to public attention and helped find a solution.

Wild man Sutch also backed British beef throughout the mad cow disease crisis, saying: 'I've been eating it for years and look at me!'

The late Sir Patrick Moore, TV astronomer, was the OMRLP finance minister for a short time. He once summed up the party perfectly: 'The Official Monster Raving Loony Party had an advantage over all other political parties in that they *knew* they were loonies.' If only the major parties today had the same honesty.

I first encountered David Sutch in the early sixties when he fronted his rock band Screaming Lord Sutch and the Savages. Many great musicians, such as guitarist Ritchie Blackmore, passed through their ranks and they were like no other band I'd ever seen. Sutch wore a cloak and had fangs dripping with blood, and the whole performance was dramatic and theatrical. Girls in the audience used to pass out at the sight of him. He predated Alice Cooper by a good ten years. My first band, the Rockin' Phantoms, used to include two Sutch live classics in our act, 'I'm a Hog for You Baby' and 'Jack the Ripper'. Excellent titles, huh?

Sutch died in 1999 but the Monster Raving Loony Party goes on. I've threatened my family for years that I'll sign up as a candidate, mirrored top hat and all. I'd fit right in, as each word of the party title describes me perfectly.

Two of their ideas I'm certainly going to nick for my own manifesto:

One is to divert the Channel tunnel to Jersey so making the whole of the United Kingdom an offshore tax haven. Genius!

My other favourite is the ballot paper design for the referendum as to whether we stay in Europe or not...

> Please Tick ONE of the following:
> a) IN
> b) OUT
> c) SHAKE IT ALL ABOUT

Only recently, a guy called David Laurence Bishop (also known as Lord Biro) stood as candidate for the Bus-Pass Elvis Party. You wouldn't think he had a chance, but he beat the Lib Dem candidate! The council by-election was in Clifton North, Nottingham, and Lord Biro canvassed for votes in a full Elvis costume, from his jumpsuit period (why do impersonators always do Vegas Elvis?) with big gold belt, jewel-encrusted sunglasses, the lot. The Lib Dems took the humiliating defeat in good humour. A spokesman was quoted as saying they were 'all shook up' by the result.

Were people just voting for a pensioner in an Elvis costume in protest at what the other parties have to offer? Who knows, but his proposed policies included plans to tighten laws on handgun ownership and legalize brothels, giving a 30 per cent discount to OAPs. He got the male senior citizen vote at least.

*

So, on the basis that nuttier things have happened I'm going to concentrate on giving you a chance to consider placing your vote for 'Noddy Holder's Mama We're All Crazee Now Party' (NHMWACN). I reckon we will pull in a fair few votes. Just wait until you get to grips with my manifesto (as I said to the wife last night).

There's a lot of bollocks spouted once politics is up for discussion. Let me state right at the start that I'm pretty much of the opinion that when anyone gets into a position of power over others, they are more than likely to fall victim to some sort of scandal or corruption. We'll be stamping that out right away.

Western society has got itself tied up in knots attempting to dictate how people live every nanosecond of their lives. My basic philosophy is that we are not as stupid as politicians make us out to be. There is a need to simplify bureaucracy, so we all understand the workings of the country and hopefully everybody will contribute their fair share. I know human nature dictates otherwise, with greed, envy and laziness coming into play, but I'm sure 99 per cent of people are born good and, left to their own devices, most folk will do the right thing in any given situation. The more rules and regulations are introduced the more difficult issues become. It's like the ancient story of the Native American chief, Two Eagles. There are a few variations on the tale but the gist of it is as follows:

An old Indian chief sits around a campfire on the reservation, smoking a ceremonial pipe of peace and eyeing two US government officials there to interview him.

One government official asks, 'Chief Two Eagles, you've known the white man for ninety years – his wars and his technological advances, his progress, and the damage he does.'

The chief nods in agreement.

The official continues, 'Considering all this, in your opinion, where does the white man go wrong?'

The chief stares at the government officials for over a minute and then calmly replies, 'When white man finds land, Indians own it. Freedom, no taxes, no debt, plenty buffalo and deer, plenty beaver, clean water, medicine man no charge, Indian man spend all day hunting and fishing, all night have sex . . .'

The chief leans back and smiles. 'Only white man is dumb enough to think he can improve system like that.'

It would have been great to have Chief Two Eagles as my deputy prime minister. One day a naive young Native American brave came to Chief Two Eagles's wigwam and asked how the old man got such a great name. 'Well,' said the Chief, 'it follows our custom that, when a new child is born, the father goes outside and the first thing he sees becomes the child's name. When I was born, the first thing my father saw were two eagles flying across the sky, so that became my name. When my first son was born, the first thing I saw was a deer running into the forest, so my son became Running Deer. With my daughter, it was raining hard, and therefore she was named Passing Cloud. Tell me, why do you ask such a question, Two Dogs Shagging?'

My smile is just a frown turned upside down.

So let's get started. You can't do a thing unless the financial situation is under control so let's tackle that first.

Economy:
'Annual income twenty pounds, annual expenditure nineteen and six, result happiness. Annual income twenty pounds, annual expenditure twenty pounds ought and six, result misery.' So says Mr Micawber in *David Copperfield*.

My dad never had a bank account as he never had any money left over each week to put into one anyway. He drummed into me as a kid that the money paid out should never exceed the money coming in. Whether it's your household expenses or a company account, don't spend more than you earn – simple sums. This applies to the budget of the country as well.

The national debt runs to billions: we've mortgaged the country over and over, and our children's future along with it. I can't begin to see how we can suddenly find several billion in loose change down the back of the country's collective sofa, unless we suddenly unearth vast gold deposits underneath Grimsby. We could make a start on doing things properly by at least balancing our incomings and our outgoings.

For a start we could try to concentrate on our own business instead of spending all our time poking our nose into everyone else's. Quite why we think we have the right to dictate how people in other countries conduct their affairs is a mystery to me. Where do we get off in being such infernal busybodies? No wonder we never win the Eurovision Song Contest anymore. Nil points!

Right, keeping our noses out should save us a few bob. Russia has dismissed us as just a small island to which no one pays any attention, and Chinese newspaper *Global Times* reported, 'The UK is not a big power in the eyes of the Chinese. It is just an old European country apt for travel and study.' This last statement is not true, of course: other nationalities waste no time in taking advantage of our amenities. My friends around the world tell me Britain is seen now as a soft touch, so we have to face up to the fact that Britannia no longer rules the waves and we have to change our image, and quickly. My policy is to get our own house in order with education, health-care and the economy, otherwise we will not be in any condition to help ourselves let alone anyone else.

I stand up for helping where there is poverty and suffering. I'm not advocating we turn our back on all places that need assistance, but there are many parts of the world where our money, given in all good faith, does not reach those for whom it is intended. I'd rather each person chose for themselves where to donate their cash, rather than have the government decide who it thinks is deserving, often by ducking and diving with some gun-toting warlord.

If I can leave a bit more money in the pockets of workers, they will be generous. You only have to watch campaigns like Comic Relief and Children in Need to see the massive amount of support the public have for deserving causes. Still, most charities at home are suffer-ing but only a very few get massive TV coverage; the rest have to rely on conscientious, hard-working individuals to continually raise funds.

Okay, on to taxation. Yes, a tricky one. I'd give the whole system an overhaul. How can it be fair that you get taxed at least three times on the same money? You get taxed when you earn the money, and you get taxed again on the interest if you're able to invest some of that money. You buy a house, therefore paying stamp duty, another tax. You pay VAT, yet another form of tax, on most things you buy every day. Even when you are dead the taxman comes after you to grab back even more from what you've left to your loved ones. Boo, hiss! He's behind you!

> *Now my advice for those who die, declare the*
> *pennies on your eyes.*

Health and Education

I'm a huge supporter of both the National Health Service and the state school system. However, if people wish to pay privately for what they consider to be more exclusive education or healthcare, they have an absolute right to do so. It is their money to spend as they please, but I will point out, it isn't necessarily the case that just because you are paying they are any better in quality. Never assume either state schools or National Health centres and hospitals are inferior to their private counterparts.

Health and education labour under the weight of endless demands from government officials, councils, managers, middle managers, accountants, pen pushers and know-it-alls, most of whom have never worked as teachers or nurses. This has now created an environment where in both hospitals and schools the workforce is too busy trying to fulfil quotas and fill out corresponding paperwork, leaving not enough time for the down-to-earth tasks of keeping the wards clean and teaching children to read a book.

I'd cut back on all those 'looking over the shoulder' roles. Get teachers, doctors and nurses properly trained, pay them a decent amount of money for such important jobs, then let them be supervised by experienced mentors. I'd encourage long-serving staff members to share their years of expertise by advising my new government. Matrons not managers, teachers not telltales. No more 'Death by Clipboard', and no more will kids be missing out on huge areas of education because the only things valued are those that get an Ofsted tick.

Foreign Policy
As I've said, my main foreign policy would be to keep out of things that don't concern us!

However, I do believe there are many things we could learn from other nations if we weren't so arrogant to believe we were already the best at everything. We need to drop the British imperialist attitude and get rid of the terrible reputation abroad that we are all just pissed-up, sunburnt lager louts and flesh-flashing floozies. There is a train of thought that Brits behave like this because we are the one European country where most people don't speak a second language. Brits can have difficulty communicating abroad, and as they are embarrassed when ordering food or being out of their comfort zone, they become louder as a cover up. Behaviour abroad does not alter the fact that the same thing happens nightly every weekend in every city centre in the UK. I've a suspicion it probably has something to do with what comes in a bottle or a glass.

Wide eyed and legless.

Talking of booze, I have a bee in my bonnet with wine snobs who get very huffy if you question them. Once I was in a really posh London restaurant for a friend's sixtieth birthday treat, and we duly ordered the meal and a couple of bottles of very expensive wine. The waiter poured me a small taster. Now I am no connoisseur, but even I know when wine is not as it should be. The smell reminded me of Dave Hill's socks after we had been on stage for two hours and the taste was even worse. The waiter was having none of it...

'Thees iz how it should taste, monsieur,'...as his face curled up after taking a sip himself.

I told him to open the other bottle to see if that too was corked. It was just as bad, obviously the whole case of wine had been tainted somehow, but this stroppy French sommelier would not accept the fact, and began to give me some arrogant Gallic lip. Bad move on his part. Staff at these posh places do sometimes think they can bully you and look down their noses, but my money is as good as anybody's. I'd kept my cool up until then, but my voice was starting to increase in volume, and when that happens the whole room begins to notice. Those Slade songs didn't sound like they did for no reason.

'I wouldn't even put this cat's piss on my pommes frites, monsieur,' I barked. Snottyman's superior air was now deflating rapidly because I was standing up to him. The maîtresse d' came running over, was very nice and very apologetic, and calmed the situation, as all eyes turned from our table back to their own conversations.

I was just about to pinch a quote from Dame Edith Evans – 'This place has gorne arwfff terribly' – but the rest of the evening went without a hitch. You can take the boy out of the Black Country …

If you like red wine and don't like white and you are eating fish, take no notice of the etiquette: drink red, even have it chilled if that's how *you* like it – it's your money. A friend told me that those trips folk make over the English Channel to Calais to stock up on cheaper wine are a waste of time. The stores put out the rubbish that the French wouldn't touch with a bargepole. The English lap it up, thinking they have a bargain.

Anyway, we can still find a lot 'over there' to inspire us.

German schools continue to have proper apprentice-ships for kids, teaching blue-collar work skills, which is much better than channelling every kid towards university. The backbone of German industry is built on family businesses, who take a long-term view rather than the fastest turnover of profit. They are good on quality as well as price. We could do that. We have the skills and could re-establish our reputation. 'British-made' still has the solid ring to it around the world and we could easily capitalize on that.

In Germany, France and many other European countries, if you have children you are subsidized and childcare is less expensive that it is here. This means parents have more of a choice as to whether they continue their careers or stay home to bring up their children. Giving people the right to choose would bring more of a balance to the benefits to society of both options. They have far less emphasis in Europe on home-buying than we do here. They are more than happy to rent and don't get themselves bogged down with crippling mortgages, so they have spare cash that gets ploughed back into the economy.

Germany has millions of citizens who in recent history lived under communist rule, and they know firsthand that it was not nice. They were liberated, and that's why they appreciate what they have got now and value their country far more. During the anti-G8 protests in the UK a couple of years ago, when rioting broke out on the streets, the police were trying to calm down an explosive situation in London. A demonstrator was angrily throwing stones and shouting at cops, 'This is what happens in a police state.'

A local shopkeeper, his store getting trashed by ignorant looters, shouted back, 'No, it ain't, mate. In a police state, they'd shoot you.'

We have to big up the good things in our own country more and be proud of it, but without being arrogant.

So my foreign policy is simple. Let's rebuild, work hard and keep out of trouble as much as possible. We won't get stuck on the coat tails of America when it argues with everyone else in the world. We'll be all nicey-nicey to other nations in the hope they will be nice back. We'll kiss some ass, pinch all their good ideas that have already been proved effective and do them better.

Home Affairs
If the system gave kids hope for the future and led to a profession, then many of the problems that hamper society would be prevented so we wouldn't have to find so many cures.

We will be bringing in much stricter deterrents and punishments for habitual offenders of crime, making prison as unattractive as possible. There'll be no softly-softly approach, especially when the crime concerns violence towards children or pensioners, and those unable to defend themselves. When nice folk reach old age they do not want to be constantly terrified and isolated in their own home, or scared to go out on the streets shopping. Cosy Parliament seems to have no idea what is going on in many areas of the country.

The NHMWACN Party will not pussyfoot around. We declare that all offenders convicted twice or more will be shipped to the same remote island way out to sea and left there to fend for themselves. These cowards will be able to beat the shit out of one another for a change, and get a taste of their own medicine. I can't come up with a better deterrent that will get through to these lowlifes.

Too much target setting is slowing down our police officers and getting them stuck behind desks instead of out on the streets. It's not the police's fault if the pendulum of political correctness has swung too much in favour of the 'rights' of everyone except the victim of a crime. Bop a burglar on the head if you meet him creeping up your stairs one night and he'll sue you for assault, *and* be awarded a compensation payout equal to a lottery win. My party will put the victims of crime first and if you are a criminal who gets injured in any way while committing your crime of choice...tough shit!

Still, as far as I am aware in this country, you are innocent of any crime until *proven* guilty. We seem to have lost sight of that. The media splash the names of the accused, including those not even charged with offences, all over their front pages and then the big gobs take to social media to vent their opinion despite knowing none of the facts. Enough already. Your vote for me will mean only people actually charged with a crime can be publically named. No one but those involved will have the right to comment and if the accused are found innocent by a court of law everyone has to accept the verdict. This is what's called Democracy with a capital D. Commenting both in the media and on social networks as if the verdict was wrong, as happens now, will be severely dealt with.

Our Charter will state that being a 'jobsworth', whatever your profession, will be a sackable offence. Those who *think* they are in positions of authority and power (you know who you are!) will only be rewarded for the occasions where they show common sense and apply rational thought. All those obsessed with ridiculous rules and other politically correct bullshit ... you're fired!

National Security and Intelligence
(... or lack of it)

Once I am appointed prime minister and privy to all national secrets, I'll have an open mind and it will take a lot to shock me. I'm pretty convinced we're not told the half of what actually goes on in the world. If I found out that contact had been made with aliens from other planets it wouldn't surprise me in the least. I was a disbeliever at one time but I had a 'nearly close' encounter once. Well, not actually with an alien being, but a flying saucer. I did! Honestly, it's completely true, I saw an actual UFO.

A while ago I was staying in a hotel room high up on cliffs on the south coast, with floor-to-ceiling windows looking out over the sea. It was midnight and I was sitting in an armchair near the window reading a newspaper. Suzan had gone off to the bathroom to get ready for bed. (What *do* women do in the bathroom that takes so long before going to bed? Answers on a postcard please.) Suddenly the whole room was illuminated in dazzling white light. First off, I thought it was a police helicopter, with its spotlight sweeping the beach looking for drug takers, which happens around that area sometimes. I can sense your scepticism as you're reading this. Well, let me tell you, I had a perfect view, and I'd only had one drink, well, maybe two.

Accelerating across the night sky was this huge circular craft, the shape we've always seen in movies and books, with blinding beams shooting out from all around. There was only a faint whirring sound, but it was travelling so fast that the downthrust was causing huge waves to break on to the shore, just as if there was a storm. I was screaming for Suzan to come and see quickly. I think she thought I was having a funny turn. She raced out of the bathroom, but by that time the spaceship had disappeared over the horizon. I was telling her what had happened and she said, 'You've had a drink, dropped off to sleep and dreamt it, you silly sod.'

Anyway, I sat next to the window for another couple of hours looking at the sky. Suzan got up from bed: 'What are you doing? It's not going to come back, Spacecraft are not like buses. Do you think there'll be another one along in a minute, and it's going to land, and some little man with big eyes and an aerial on his head will invite you on board for a chat?'

I said, 'You never know, the aliens might be looking for the perfect member of the human species to study.'

She rolled her eyes, muttered something about an ego the size of a planet and went back to bed in a huff.

Anyway, next morning when we woke up, I switched on the TV to the national news. There had been hundreds of reported sightings at around midnight of a UFO travelling in a straight line from Gloucester and along the south coast. I was elated ... 'See, see, I told you I wasn't imagining it. Loads of other people saw it too.'

The Ministry of Defence gave out some cover-up statement that it was a meteor shower. Absolute rubbish!

Why am I including this story in my manifesto? Well, it's obvious, isn't it? If aliens were to land, everyone knows the first thing they would say is 'Take me to your leader' so if that was me, you'd want to know I could handle it, wouldn't you?

Of course, I can't take on the role of Supreme Leader without a suitable team around me. I've rummaged around a few booze cabinets in my time, but let me now unveil to you the 'Noddy Holder's Mama We're All Crazee Now' ministerial cabinet.

PRIME MINISTER (or I quite like SUPREME LEADER): NODDY HOLDER (of course)

A thoroughly reliable individual who wants to . . .

Bring you sunshine with a smile.

HOME AFFAIRS: MRS BROWN

Irish mammy Mrs Brown's ability to run a home is second to none. Her methods may be chaotic and unorthodox, but it's all done with love and she holds her diverse family together no matter what. I reckon this system could be scaled up, so the country is run along similar lines. I'm sure Brendan O'Carroll wouldn't mind wearing a dress and cardigan permanently for the greater good.

FOREIGN AFFAIRS: KARL PILKINGTON

A former work colleague from my radio days, Karl is a globetrotter who has visited many weird and wonderful places. He is rarely impressed and his own quirky philosophy of life would have the cabinet meetings in uproar. How could any diplomat resist that little, perfectly round face?

CHANCELLOR OF THE EXCHEQUER: GENE SIMMONS (of Kiss)

Gene is a shrewd cookie. He emigrated from Israel to the USA, and through hard work, dedication and madcap make-up, he's lived the American Dream as an entrepreneur. With a drink- and drug-free brain, unusual for a rock 'n' roller or many of those cocaine-fuelled Wall St whizz kids, he is said to be worth $300 million. People *think* he's crazy, so he fits the character profile we need on our team.

EDUCATION: CAITLIN MORAN

A brilliant example of home schooling, Caitlin is a journalist, novelist and broadcaster who, as a youngster, used local libraries to teach herself. She's a mother, a music lover and a modern thinker and hails from my old stomping ground of Wolverhampton. I have told her she could be my lovechild. As a young man hanging out in the town, I had a bike and got around a bit!

HEALTH: ANNE HEGERTY ('The Governess' from ITV's The Chase)

Anne certainly looks like an old-fashioned, ample-bosomed ward matron. She might not be as cuddly as

Hattie Jacques from the *Carry On* movies but Anne's no-nonsense style would get those hospitals shipshape in no time. Can you imagine getting a bed bath from her? You'd get better immediately just to avoid it, or perhaps not...Whatever turns you on!

SPORT: BRADLEY WIGGINS AND KARREN BRADY

Anyone who can ride a bike that fast, while sporting 'Noddy Holder-style' sideburns, has to be a reliable bloke. Just think of the drag effect Bradley Wiggins had to overcome. He's also a snappy dresser, which goes a long way with me. You can always tell the man from his wardrobe.

Karren Brady is tried and tested. She was the first female boss of any football club, after instigating the buying of Birmingham City FC. When she travelled on the team coach for the first time, one of the confrontational players came out with, 'Hey, guv, I can see your tits through that top.'

Karren calmly replied, 'Well, when I transfer you to Crewe you won't be able to see them so well from there.'

This is the attitude we want in the cabinet.

ARTS AND CULTURE: FRANK SKINNER

Frank and I speak the same language. 'Yow want the job, Frank? It'll be bostin', our kid.' He'll be in charge of Black Country and Birmingham dialects (they're *not* the same) becoming the compulsory second languages of the nation.

A braindead TV reviewer once wrote about the Midlands accents as sounding like the batteries are running out on the voicebox and you want to rush to replace them. He won't think he's being so funny when he's made to speak like me.

Frank's a comedian, an Elvis fan and he likes proper art. That's culture sorted then. He can have Dappy (from N-Dubz) as his assistant to advise on all things 'yoof'.

LAW AND ORDER: ALEX FERGUSON

His 'hairdryer treatment' of bawling out footballers could be usefully employed on criminals. If he can have multi-millionaire footballers quaking in their boots, let's get him across into the justice system. If he wants to transfer all convicts to Belarus, so be it.

POLITICAL CORRECTNESS WATCHDOG: KEITH LEMON

I can't think of anyone more un-PC than Keith. Therefore it will be his designated role to puncture all silly, stuffy, political-correctness-gone-mad scenarios. He has no fear so will catch some of the more toffee-nosed dignitaries off guard. I think with his particular look he could also be another lovechild of mine.

INTER-GALACTIC RELATIONS: PALOMA FAITH

As a space cadet she'll be on permanent standby to assist me with any communication received of an alien nature. If anyone can put visitors from another galaxy at ease, and avert an extraterrestrial incident, it's Paloma.

PUBLIC RELATIONS OFFICERS: NOEL AND LIAM GALLAGHER

Whenever the press need interviews or quotes I'd put up one, or both, of these two. Their interviews are hilarious. They would never spout any propaganda: they'd tell it exactly as it is. They may punch reporters or each other in the process. So be it.

I've chosen these ministers because they are all strong characters who lead and don't just follow the herd without questioning.

> *Do not follow where the path may lead. Go instead where there is no path and leave a trail.*
>
> Ralph Waldo Emerson

Here are a few more party proposals we hope to get through Parliament when we are elected.

I will put forward plans to build a new zoo and theme park based on the celebrity/reality TV show culture. One idea is to have a rollercoaster ride built from Katie Price's discarded breast implants. Oh, what thrills will be in store! Instead of cages there will be see-through plastic houses, where spectators are able to watch the everyday antics of 'celebs' like Joey Essex and Kerry Katona. We will see them having their spray tans, hair extensions and Botox treatments. It won't be too long before we see these fame addicts conceiving and giving birth. This is not an invasion of privacy as they are quite willing to show all on TV and in magazines.

I once had a TV crew, who were filming a series about the day-to-day life of Katona, come knocking on my front door to ask if I would go along with her to a tattoo parlour, where we would get matching designs. I have never even met the woman. My reply, as is usual in these kind of situations, was gentle but firm... 'FUUUUUCK OOOOFF!'

It used to be rebellious to get a tattoo. Now everybody seems to have at least one, so I suppose that means it's rebellious not to have one.

I am going to ban all film musicals that employ actors and actresses who cannot sing and are contracted just because they are famous and put bums on seats. As far as I'm concerned, the perfect example of this was the film version of *Mamma Mia!* I know it is one of the most 'Money, Money, Money' making movies ever in Britain, and I know the stage show is fab. My friends all loved the film and were urging me to see it, so off I went, expecting to be knocked out. Don't get me wrong, I love Abba music and I knew them back in the day, but I came out of the cinema thinking this was an irretrievable waste of two hours of my life. Cast musical talent, there's plenty around, and get a much better end result. Quality can fill cinemas.

On the subject of singing, I'm fed up of hearing some newcomers showing off how many notes they can attempt in a minute. This will be prohibited on the grounds that it is a public disturbance. Stick to the bloody tune – it was written like that for a reason. By all means give your interpretation, but wailing all over the place is just a cover up. You're not fooling anyone. You may think you can outdo Mariah Carey's vocal histrionics, but she can also sing a melody in tune and on time. My favourite Christmas song (other than Slade, of course) is Mariah's 'All I Want for Christmas Is You'. I think that alone has earned her the right to use her famous line: 'I don't do stairs!'

Look out for our slogan coming soon ...

A VOTE FOR NODDY HOLDER'S MAMA WE'RE ALL CRAZEE NOW PARTY IS A VOTE TO 'LOOK TO THE FUTURE NOW...IT'S ONLY JUST BEGUN'.

You know it makes sense.

Chapter Ten

WE'LL MEET AGAIN

In 2014 Dame Vera Lynn became the oldest artist, at ninety-seven years old, to have an album in the charts. There's hope for us all. 'We'll Meet Again', her most famous song and a wartime anthem, was originally released in 1940 and on sales would have been a No. 1 record if the charts had existed then. I met Dame Vera years ago and she was warm, friendly and not at all phased by a loud scallywag from rock 'n' roll land.

In the showbiz part of my world, I have come across hundreds of different personalities over the past fifty years. I've met them at TV shows, radio shows, charity fundraisers, sporting events, awards ceremonies, parties, gigs, hotels and even out shopping. Some of the famous faces are just as you imagine them to be. Some are not at all what you expect, for better or worse, but that's life.

Some you strike up a rapport with and keep in touch. It's difficult when jetting all over the globe, but even if it's a year between seeing one another, sometimes when you do meet up again it's as if it were yesterday.

*Don't know where, don't know when, but I know
we'll meet again some sunny day ...*

I got to meet many artists during my years as a radio presenter. I was one of only two people to interview Sir George Martin, the Beatles producer, when he released an instrumental album a few years back. We had met in the distant past and I decided not to just concentrate on his years with the Beatles, as these had been well documented over and over. I know myself how hard it can be coming up with diverse topics in interviews and it's always refreshing if someone tries a different approach. I knew of Sir George's classical background and his work producing comedy records, all this before being the only man who would take a chance on signing the band that became the biggest ever. He also had success post-Fab Four with bands like America (of 'A Horse with No Name' fame), so the interview covered a wide spectrum and we both enjoyed it immensely. It made for a great broadcast.

As with Dame Vera, George is from a generation where they have nothing to prove and are at ease with their achievements. From that era too came Norman Wisdom,

Frankie Howerd, Bob Monkhouse, Bruce Forsyth and Ken Dodd – I have met them all. These guys had one thing in common, besides being funny: they have the word 'APPLAUSE' running through them like a stick of seaside rock. It's all they ever wanted to hear.

I met Norman Wisdom a few times and he was a gentleman, though if there were people around he *had* to perform. The comedian Frank Carson was the same. I first saw Norman on stage in pantomime at the Birmingham Hippodrome in 1950. He was Buttons in *Cinderella* and it was my very first experience of live theatre. Norman was fast becoming a huge star, the biggest in Britain. His performance included dancing, playing instruments and doing slapstick comedy, the perfect vehicle for his talent as an all-round entertainer. Nevertheless, the showstopper for me was when he sat alone in a small spotlight in the middle of the stage, having lost the heart of Cinderella to Prince Charming, and sang a tear-jerking ballad. There was not a dry eye in the house. How often do you see that happen today? I was four years old but I can still remember the impact as if it was yesterday; it was magical. This was obviously the blueprint Norman used when he wrote and recorded his biggest hit, 'Don't Laugh at Me 'Cause I'm a Fool' a few years later. It was the first time I witnessed what it was possible to do with a live audience, laughter one minute, heartache the next.

My first meeting with Norman was on the Isle of Man, where he lived for many years. I told him the panto story and how much it meant to me, which he loved. We both received 'Tie Wearer of the Year' awards at a ceremony together one year, and the last time we met up was at a *This is Your Life* reunion TV special. The recording took place in an old building with a steep marble staircase leading to the arena. The missus and I followed Norman up the stairs to the top, when all of a sudden he started flailing about as if he was having a heart attack. He fell backwards, gambolling down the staircase, past lots of other guests. He landed in a heap at the bottom and lay there very still. Everybody was in a state of shock, then panic, shouting and running to his slumped body. We should have known better. Suddenly up he got and did his famous 'Mr Grimsdale' swaying about, coupled with his trademark hysterical laughter. Everyone was relieved and you had to laugh along with him.

This was a man in his eighties, still able to do an acrobatic fall down a flight of stairs and get up unscathed, just to get a laugh from the crowd. He'd been doing it all his life, it was second nature. Right up until he was dying, Norman would abscond from his nursing home and could be found entertaining, wearing his pyjamas, on the local garage forecourt. They sure don't make 'em like that anymore.

I'm always telling the family, 'That's what you'll be doing to me. Dragging me back home, dressed in my Santa suit, after doing a routine in the local shopping centre.'

Their reply: 'We do that already, you silly old fool!'

Nowhere could you get that happy feeling, when you are stealing that extra bow.

As I've said earlier, on my passport, for occupation I've always had 'artiste'. Please note the 'e'. That covers a multitude of sins including 'piss'.

With music, comedy, drama, dancing, performers can take you to another place for a couple of hours and I'm lucky that in my time I've had a go at all of these. Well, perhaps not dance as yet, even though the wife keeps badgering me to do *Strictly Come Dancing*. I bumped into Lulu on the street when she was doing the show, and asked her how she was coping. Now Lulu is my age and fit, fit, fit. She said it was the hardest thing she'd ever taken on physically, with rehearsing five days a week plus the two live shows at the weekend.

I was in the bar at the BBC, after me and the wife were lucky enough to be invited to a couple of the shows. Suzan was ecstatic, as we were talking to the professional dancers Karen Hardy and Lilia Kopylova, or as I called her, 'Kopyalegover'. They were encouraging me to take part in the next series after we'd had a twirl around the bar. Lilia said, 'You've got great rhythm. I'll look after you and get your dancing up to scratch. It's all just fun.' TV presenter Dominic Littlewood, who had been her dance partner the year before, was there and pointed at his glass of red wine: 'Just fun, sure. You see that, that's the blood she took from me every week.'

I think I'm a bit too long in the tooth for the show now. I'll stick to doing my Fred Astaire impersonations after a couple of gins.

I'm putting on my top hat, tying up my white tie, brushing off my tails.

I've never left my heart in San Francisco, but I have left my phone number.

One night I'm walking back to my hotel in the city, at around 10.30 p.m., and an excited crowd is gathered on the pavement outside a small theatre. I looked up at the marquee over the entrance and there was the name of some play starring Al Pacino. Now, here was a favourite actor of mine and the star of some classic seventies movies. The crowd were obviously backing up from the stage door to catch a glimpse of the man himself and maybe get autographs.

I thought, I'll hang around, I'm not in any hurry and I'll get to see Al in the flesh. I'm standing there waiting and this guy comes over, whom I recognize as the barman from my hotel situated just up the road. I always make a point of getting friendly with hotel barmen. A few dollars tip sometimes means their hand can slip accidentally when measuring a drink out. I like that. Anyway, he's on his break and asks what I'm up to.

I tell him: 'I just want to catch a glimpse of Pacino.'

He says: 'There's no need to hang around here, he'll be in the bar for a nightcap later. I'll introduce you.' Now that was a good plan.

Half an hour later Pacino strolls into the bar on his own, no fanfares. He's got a baseball cap pulled down over his eyes so you wouldn't instantly recognize him if you passed him on the street, until he opens his mouth. The voice we've all heard so many times in the movies. He pulls up a stool at the bar and the barman, true to his word, calls me over and introduces me.

'Can I buy you a drink, Mr Pacino?'

I'd made him an offer he couldn't refuse, so he invited me to sit down and chat. We spent the next couple of hours discussing film, music and TV, and the parallels of how the bosses in our different industries were now mostly money men who were stifling a lot of new creativity. As happens on these occasions we said we'd catch up when he was next in London. I left him my number, but I haven't had the call as yet! Still, I got to meet 'The Godfather'. Cool or what?

Talking about *The Godfather* and San Francisco, this was the city for Slade's last ever concert together. We were special guests on a bill with Ozzy Osbourne. His wife Sharon was managing Slade over in America at the time, and I've known her since she was a teenager. Sharon's dad, the late Don Arden, was the self-proclaimed god-father of music management and I spent many a good night at parties down at their home in Wimbledon. I got on well with him, he could be a teddy bear, but you crossed him at your peril. Sharon learned all the tricks of the trade from her dad, and lots more besides when she eventually went into management herself.

I've known Black Sabbath, Ozzy's original band, since Birmingham in the sixties. We were all playing the same circuit alongside musicians like Robert Plant and John Bonham, Roy Wood, Jeff Lynne, The Spencer Davis Group with Steve Winwood, and The Moody Blues. These are just the tip of the iceberg of what the Midlands music scene has produced over the last five decades, even though it never gets recognized as a major music melting pot.

There have been many drinking sessions with Ozzy, and he is a funny, funny man, plus we did have the added bonus of being able to understand one another's accents. He and Sharon would come round for dinner and it wasn't unusual for him to end up passed out with his face in his meal. The kids couldn't believe it.

Black Sabbath had to make the difficult decision of sacking Ozzy in the late seventies because of his excesses, and this sent him on an even worse downward spiral. Sharon rescued him from the brink of self-destruction, took hold of him, got his shit together and guided him to become one of the world's biggest rock attractions with an outrageous image to go along with the success.

I'm one of the few who could stay the course drinking with the comical 'Prince of Darkness'. A favourite trick of his was to get a victim paralytic drunk, wait for them to pass out and then shave off their eyebrows, or just the one depending what mood he was in. In the late eighties Don Powell, Slade's drummer, and Ozzy would go to Alcoholics Anonymous meetings together, only to leave just in time to catch last orders in the pub!

One night the three of us had a long session after hours in a regular watering hole in north London, not far from where they both lived. The owners finally wanted their beauty sleep so Ozzy said, 'Let's get a cab and you can drop me at the start of the M1, I'm going to hitchhike up to Birmingham.'

I answered, 'What the fuck are you talking about? It's the middle of the night and it's pouring with rain.'

He said, 'Well, I can't go home, Sharon will kill me. We were supposed to be going out for a meal.'

'Don't worry, Sharon's used to you rolling in late and drunk. She'll calm down.'

Oz still looked scared, 'Yeah... but it's her birthday!'

'What?... Oh no, you're up shit creek without a paddle.'

All three of us were very, very inebriated and Oz insisted, 'You two have got to come home with me and take the blame for keeping me out.'

So we got a cab and arrived at the Osbourne house. We were trudging up the drive when all of a sudden all the security lights came blazing on. Sharon opened an upstairs window and screamed some colourful expletives at us, as only she can. There was a shotgun in her hand so we took off like rabbits and she let go with both barrels. Luckily it was the side of their car that got riddled with pellet holes.

It was not so long after that a big scare happened. Ozzy tried to strangle Sharon and nearly killed her. The next day, locked up in jail, he didn't even know what he'd done. I'd bollocked him many times for frightening Sharon when he was in a chaotic state, but this was a wake-up call for all of us to slow down on the partying.

The Osbournes have survived all that life has thrown at them, good and bad, and have a bond now that is stronger than ever.

I generally get on with other frontmen, as we have a common dilemma in that we have to soak up the flak we get from our other band members.

I've got a soft spot for Mick Hucknall, who gets a bad rap from the media. He should care, with the number of albums he's sold, and he's packed arenas all over the world for years. I was to interview him for my radio show and everyone warned me he was a difficult character. I like to make my own mind up about people, and I had a feeling we'd get along fine. I was right. I knew he'd have a musical knowledge and background I could tap into. His awkward reputation probably stemmed from the fact that most interviewers honed in on his private life, when he was still a man about town, and not on his music. His encounters with the ladies in the past probably helped with his romantic songwriting anyway. You can't write properly about something you know nothing about. We chatted about shared influences and I told him I loved his voice. He liked the fact that, at the end of the show, I said he was a kid who'd come out of the streets of Salford, earned a few bob and grown into a European man of style. Mick appreciates the finer things in life that his success has bought him, without letting go of his roots. He's still first and foremost a fine musician.

He was amongst the guests at the wedding of our mutual friends, the actress Amanda Holden and Chris

Hughes. It was being covered by a big celebrity magazine and took place at Babington House down in the West Country, just before Christmas. Suzan and I had parked up and were approaching the hotel to check in. Coming towards us were Chris and his best man, the racing driver David Coulthard.

I said, 'How are you feeling, Chris? Everything all sorted and no panic stations?'

He replied, 'Don't ask me, Amanda's in charge. I'll just get my "I do" right.' He pointed at two huge cannons either side of the doors of the little wedding chapel just across the grounds.

'What are they for?' Suzan asked.

'They are to pump out fake snow so everywhere will be covered white when we have the photos taken. No one is allowed to walk anywhere and leave footprints!'

Brilliant, and classic Amanda. She is one of the most organized people on the planet and had everything calculated with military precision. She had even got real reindeer and a sleigh to entertain the young kids.

During the service, one of Amanda's actress buddies, Rose Keegan, read out an old-fashioned article in a perfect cut-glass, upper-class accent. It was called 'How to Keep Your Husband Happy'. For example, 'When your husband comes home from work, make sure his slippers are warming by the fireside, his pipe is filled and he has a full glass of whisky next to his armchair'.

The women were all booing and the men were all cheering. It was hilarious.

Later at the wedding meal, Suzan and myself were seated at a large table, where the guests included Piers Morgan and his future wife Celia. From what I knew about him I never thought for a minute that Piers would be the sort of guy I'd get on with. He turned out to be charming and Suzan bonded with him instantly. They are both from journalistic backgrounds and spent ages swapping newsroom escapade stories.

Mick Hucknall and his lovely wife Gabriella were also seated at our table, and Piers steered the conversation on to myself and Mick, primarily to wind us up. The wine had been flowing and Piers said, 'You two would never have been able to pull so many women in the past if you hadn't been rich and famous musicians. You're hardly handsome, either of you!'

A buzz went around the other guests on the table. Had Piers gone too far this time?

I'm used to it. This wasn't the first time I'd had such an insult thrown at me.

Quick as a flash I came back with 'I never went short of female companionship before I was famous and nor, I'm sure, did Mick. It's all down to our natural charisma, our smooth way with a song and our big dicks!'

Piers held his hands up. 'Touché.'

I first met Amanda when we worked together on three

series of the TV comedy drama *The Grimleys* in the late nineties. Early mornings in make-up she would be drinking some foul-looking concoction to keep her trim and healthy. One morning she said to me: 'You should have some of this, it will do you good. Come to my dressing room and I'll make you some.'

I went down there and she'd got her juicer on the go. She poured me what can only be described as green-coloured mud, and it tasted pretty much how it looked. Off we went for our first scene of the day together. We got to the set, and let me tell you that mud shake moved through the system pretty sharpish. Not only was it foul tasting, it was foul smelling. We were both constantly breaking wind, and it was picked up on the microphones. We couldn't stop giggling and the director warned us: no more cleansing on the shoot or else.

I told my wife early on in our relationship, you'll know if it's me breaking wind in a crowd as ...

> *My farts only smell of Chanel.*
> Noddy Odour MBE

While on the subject of backsides, I was told a story by a sportsman friend who had joined a group of pop stars to record a song for charity. He was asked to do a day of promotion on TV and radio, so the record company booked a limousine to pick him up at 6 a.m., even though he lived within walking distance of the studios. Every day for a week the promotion people rang to check he knew the pick-up time and whether he needed a wake-up call or anything else. Nothing seemed too much trouble and my friend wasn't used to this sort of celebrity treatment. The promo day went fine, and that evening he was invited to the launch party. During a chat with the big boss of the record label, my mate decided to ask why it was thought necessary to send a huge car for a five-minute journey, and why the need to call him every day to check the arrangements. The boss replied, 'You have to understand, most of the artists here can't even wipe their own arses!'

This may be a slight exaggeration, but an artist's roadies can be called upon to perform all manner of tasks. In my own case I had a designated roadie to look after my top hat with mirrors. The hat had its own specially-made fortified hat box; and woe betide the roadie if it was ever lost or damaged during transportation around the world.

Probably the most unusual 'specialist' roadie I ever came across was one who got plenty of work blowing cocaine through a pipe up a rectum when an artist's nose had collapsed through too much drug abuse. Nice work if you can get it – just make sure you blow and don't suck! How's about that on your CV:

WE'LL MEET AGAIN

Tired and Emotional?
Cocaine Blower Up the Backside For Hire
All Arseholes considered.
References supplied if needed.

Beware, folks. I've had so many friends who've finally realized hard drugs were not so cool after all, but most realized far too late. Life is precious. Don't believe the hip hype.

Turn your face to sun and the shadows fall behind you.

Maori proverb

Another place where I seem to bump into well-known faces now and again is on a train. I do love travelling by train, especially off peak when it's quieter. I was on my way up to Manchester, in the middle of the day, and had a carriage to myself, or so I thought. Behind me I heard a little sneeze. I turned around and in the corner reading his newspaper was Larry Adler, an excellent musician I really admired. Adler was then in his eighties, but at one time he was the world's leading harmonica player, or as he preferred to call it, the mouth organ.

This was another chance I didn't want to pass up, so I went over and introduced myself. He recognized me, which broke the ice, and he asked me to join him for a chinwag. I think he was as interested in my music as I was his. I knew of his background playing jazz, classical and popular music since the 1920s, but I was transfixed for two hours as he told me stories about his life when he was younger in America. He'd played for Al Capone in the Prohibition era and he'd worked with Al Jolson when he was *the* star of Broadway. He'd known all the great American songbook composers, people like Cole Porter, George Gershwin, Irving Berlin and all the jazz greats. I'd grown up with this stuff from my dad's record collection so this was the best train journey ever. Larry's career is the sort I look up to – he was a virtuoso, not some spaced-out songwriter influencing the kids with their suicidal lyrics.

One thing these old-time entertainers have in common when you meet them is their sense of style. Even in maturity, and even though some may not be as wealthy as they once were, they are usually 'suited and booted' and looking sharp.

I like to think I carry this torch onwards. One of my favourite fashion designers is Vivienne Westwood. You do have to be adventurous to wear her clothes and shoes, but as you may have noticed over my career, sartorial elegance is my byword!

I love it when someone can stick two fingers up to the world and come up with something very original.

Vivienne has certainly done that. I remember back in the eighties, after her punk era, she appeared on a BBC TV talk show. She walked on to the set wearing one of her outrageous creations and high shoes. The audience were screaming with laughter, and did so even more when egged on by the presenter, Sue Lawley, during the interview. Vivienne eventually threatened to stop her clothes models coming on just to be scoffed at. She sat and took it with good grace, knowing that all those mocking her hadn't got a clue what she was all about.

She's now got stores in major cities all over the world and is an important export for the UK. Who's laughing now?

It's strange how anyone a bit out of the ordinary gets ridiculed just for how they look. I've had it all my life, but it's water off a duck's back to me. I just smile sweetly.

I make no apologies at all for the way I dress. Quite frankly these days people usually comment favourably, even if it makes them smile. This does seem now to be my role in life. My mates take the mickey, but I have no qualms at all about carrying a 'man bag' – in fact I've always carried a 'man bag', even before it was called a 'man bag'. Who did start calling it a 'man bag' anyway? Phone, wallet, notebook, pen, all spoil the cut of your jib, so you have to find a stylish solution.

Mark Radcliffe and I were once having a breakfast meeting, going over the arrangements for our up-and-coming talk tour, and we both happened to have shoulder bags with us. That morning we both had aching muscles in our backs as well. (I never thought before, but could it be from carrying heavy shoulder bags?) For a brief silly moment we were going to call the tour 'The Man Bags and the Bad Backs Tour', to the tune of 'Handbags and Gladrags'.

One of the more bizarre items we discussed on Mark's radio show one evening was how many pairs of shoes the average man owns. We all know that ladies love buying shoes, but what about men? A newspaper article, after research, said it was four pairs including trainers. From the listeners phoning in this seemed to be about right. Mark, though, reckoned he had about eight pairs, but me, not afraid to show my feminine side, I have lots, lots more. In fact, sixty-three more.

Mine come in all shapes and colours. I have boots for every occasion, even cowboy boots that I bought in the States on my first trip there in the seventies. They're great for when it snows. I've still got a pair of Anello & Davide genuine Cuban-heeled Beatle boots that I saved for a year to buy in the early sixties. I have various colours of brogues, some given to me by manufacturers over the years. I have blue suede shoes (uh-huh-huh), red suede, green suede, stripy, leopard skin and polka dot, and hardly a day goes by that someone doesn't say to me, 'Where did you get those shoes?' Is it a fetish?

Could be. My missus says I'm worse than any woman when it comes to shoes. I'm also a legs man when it comes to admiring women. I can tell how sexy a lady is by her shoes and the way she walks. I've rarely got it wrong.

You can always tell a person's personality from their footwear. The actor Alec Guinness always said, when getting into character, the first thing he did was find the shoes and then the walk. My leather shoes are always polished, which comes from my dad's Army influence.

Slade were the first band to wear platform shoes on *Top of the Pops* back in the glam era. It caused a stir at the time but within months everyone wanted a pair. Platforms and flared trousers became de rigueur for any seventies night on the town. Our guitarist Dave Hill kept getting higher and higher platforms until eventually his head was in the clouds (well, maybe that wasn't just down to his boots) and he had icicles hanging from his fringed haircut.

Dave has got his feet back on the ground after a health scare a couple of years ago, and he and I have managed to put our differences aside and have a catch up now and again.

As well as shoes, I have a fine display of hats, canes, neckties, watch chains and all sorts of vintage paraphernalia.

The collection got too much for the house so I have it all stored in my old warehouse, and I can while away the hours there. I suppose it's my equivalent of a garden shed.

I wore some of my collection at a ceremony in June 2014, when I received the 'Freedom' of my hometown of Walsall. It was a fantastic evening and got me all choked up, with people regaling the Council Chamber with many memories. I adapted one of my poems about the town to read out, and I only wished my mum and dad had been alive to be there. I'm sure they were cheering me on from above. By all accounts I can now herd cows and sheep through the town centre. This could come in useful if I decide on a career change and become a shepherd. Apparently I'm also entitled to a free pint of beer in any pub in the town. I have yet to test this out.

I've had some nice awards over the years, including an MBE presented to me by Prince Charles at Buckingham Palace. I was all kitted out in a frock coat and accessories on that occasion as well.

HRH complimented me with 'Very smart, you're the best dressed man here today.'

Tell you what, he looked pretty snazzy himself in his Navy uniform. I must get me one of them cos ...

All the nice girls love a sailor.

Liverpool actor and comedian Ricky Tomlinson talked me into singing along with him on a record he was making called 'Are You Looking At Me?' He drew up a contract paying me an old shilling, a Val Doonican album and a week in his caravan. I'm still waiting for the week in his caravan.

We had a riotous time doing the record and a video in Liverpool, backed by a traditional Irish band, alongside the late great actor and musician Geoffrey Hughes and Michael Starke, another fine actor. The record charted and we did the Michael Parkinson show, where I had a catch up with Billy Connolly, whom I hadn't seen for over twenty years.

Suzan and I got invited to Ricky's wedding. The service took place in front of Ricky and Rita's family and friends, which included a host of comedians, so it was never going to be a sedate affair. For a start we were seated behind Liz Dawn (Vera Duckworth from *Coronation Street*) and impersonator Faith Brown, who was doing her best Vera impression, so we were listening to Vera in stereo.

The time came for the inevitable line – and the moment Ricky must have been dreading – 'If any man can show just cause or impediment why they may not lawfully be joined together, let him now speak, or else hereafter forever hold his peace'. Well, this opened the floodgates. What do you call a load of comedians gathered together, a gaggle or maybe a giggle? Anyway, up they all got. From all over the room came various versions of 'I know a reason', amongst them Frank Carson, Norman Collier, Stan Boardman, all shouting out. Ricky had his head in his hands.

Order was eventually restored and Ricky and Rita were suitably spliced. The speeches after the meal were always going to be hilarious, with comics taking turns to outdo one another. To top it all, the doyen of Liverpool comedy, Ken Dodd, was there as a guest. All the comics were using his jokes to tease him. It didn't matter: Doddy came on as the finale, and he's able to do four hours of material without batting an eyelid, so his wedding gags were coming thick and fast. Everybody was aching. Ken has extra funny bones.

Ricky is probably best known these days for playing layabout dad Jim Royle in TV's *The Royle Family*. This was created by my pals Craig Cash and Caroline Aherne, who are also the comedy geniuses behind BBC's *The Mrs Merton Show*. Interviewer Mrs Merton's famous line to Debbie McGee, the much younger wife of magician Paul Daniels, has become a classic: 'And so, Debbie, what was it that first attracted you to the millionaire Paul Daniels?'

Some things never change. In Jane Austen's *Pride and Prejudice*, the heroine Elizabeth is asked by her sister, 'When did you first realise you loved him?' referring to Mr Darcy.

Elizabeth replied: 'I think it was the first time I came up the drive and saw his house.'

The one thing that really makes my wife Suzan's hackles rise is the mere suggestion that she married me for my money. Mention this, even as a joke, and you would feel the full force of her tongue, as anyone who knows her will testify.

Our own wedding was a small gathering of nearest and dearest. We had been living together for fourteen years and I always say it took so long because I had to be sure. Suzan says, 'It took FOURTEEN YEARS to be sure?' Some of my more mature musician friends have been married at least five times. They are amazed that I've got away with only twice!

We were happy as we were, we had Django, but finally I came round to the idea of marriage. Suzan wanted to set things in motion, but said, 'You haven't even asked me yet. You've got to surprise me at some point with a proper proposal.' She was thinking a banner in the sky maybe or a procession down the High Street. What she got one evening, while she was doing the ironing, was 'Well, are you going to marry me or not?' My best man Swin suggested we just do a dance over some chicken bones, but Suzan wasn't impressed and was pretty sure it wouldn't be legal.

The day went without a hitch and Suzan walked down the aisle to The Ronettes' 'Be My Baby'. We had a jukebox set up so that all the guests could choose music for the dancing later.

We'd kept the wedding under wraps, but as I was about to leave to go to the service I got a phone call from a newspaper. The reporter was looking for confirmation that my wife had left me, we were getting a divorce and I was checking myself into a rehab clinic that day. I couldn't even be bothered to give an answer and gently put the phone down. I went out and had one of the best days of my life with the people who matter to me.

And I said to myself, what a wonderful world.